Where Do Conservatives and Liberals Come From?

And What Ever Happened to Life, Liberty and the Pursuit of Happiness?

Part One

THOMAS MULLEN

ISBN-13: 978-1517679415

ISBN-10: 1517679419:

For all who are trying to find their way to freedom

CONTENTS

Chapter One:

Something is Wrong with the World

"Let me tell you why you're here. You're here because you know something. What you know you can't explain, but you feel it. You've felt it your entire life, that there's something wrong with the world. You don't know what it is, but it's there, like a splinter in your mind, driving you mad. It is this feeling that has brought you to me."

– Morpheus to Neo in the motion picture "The Matrix" (1999)[1]

Back in 2010, I was invited to speak at a conference sponsored by Campaign for Liberty, a libertarian-leaning organization founded by former Congressman and presidential candidate Ron Paul. Arriving at the hotel the night before, I discovered the political conference wasn't the only convention there. The same hotel was also hosting a huge Star Wars convention.

Everywhere I looked, characters from the hit movie franchise adorned the lobby. I got a picture with Darth Vader. As it was the end of a long day, I headed to the bar for a beer. A man dressed as young Obi-Wan Kenobi sat down next to me.

"How's the convention going for you?" he asked.

"I just got here," I replied, "but I'm not here for the same convention you are. I'm here for the Campaign for Liberty event."

"What's Campaign for Liberty?" he inquired.

I looked around for a moment and replied, "Well, it's an organization everyone at your convention should want to join."

"Why is that?' he asked.

"Because they want to end the American Empire and restore the Old Republic," I replied.

The young Obi-Wan looked at me for a moment with an expression that read, "Do I really want to get into this?" Then, as if acquiescing to his own curiosity, he said "Tell me some more."

I explained the organization as briefly as I could. Occasionally, he would interject, "I actually agree with that." He seemed to agree with more than he disagreed with. Then, it was his turn.

"I'm a dyed-in-the-wool liberal," he told me.

When I asked him what that meant to him, this was his reply:

"I believe if you can afford a $400,000.00 house, then more power to you. Enjoy it. But what's wrong with this country is the idea that people feel entitled to houses they can't afford, vacations they borrow money to take and two or three cars. People need to start living within their means."

This is what a "dyed-in-the-wool liberal" thinks?

Believe it or not, I hear statements like this from people who self-identify as liberals all the time. Yet, less than a year before my new friend made this statement, President Obama had called for and then signed into law an $800 billion "stimulus package" designed to subsidize people who couldn't afford to pay their own mortgages. Obi-Wan didn't seem to notice the irony.

Liberals aren't the only ones who sometimes fail to see the difference between what they and their representatives believe.

That same year, I attended the Conservative Political Action Conference (CPAC) for the first time. CPAC is an annual rally held in Washington, D.C. where "anybody who's anybody" in conservative politics gathers to speak, promote books, launch political campaigns, etc.

In addition to an all-star cast of conservative speakers, the event also features an exhibit hall where mostly grassroots conservative organizations set up booths and ply their wares. I was as interested in what these "regular folks" had to say as in the featured speakers. I asked each of them why they identified as conservative.

Their answers weren't surprising. I heard a lot of affirmations of the free market, small government, individual liberty and religious freedom. These are the principles nearly every one associates with "conservatism."

What was surprising was how little these positions resembled those taken by the conference's speakers. On the big stage, attendees were warned that President Obama's "socialist" healthcare program, which subsidizes private insurers, threatens Medicare, a healthcare program run completely by the government.

They heard passionate cries that Obama was "gutting the military" by not increasing military spending as fast as they deemed necessary. They heard that Obama was "soft on radical Islam," and even implications he was a Muslim himself.

They heard little or nothing about rolling back regulations on business or reducing government spending. They heard no criticism of the federal government spying on their phone calls or e-mails. They heard nothing about reducing the size and reach of government at all.

Then, there is what liberal and conservative politicians actually *do*.

In 2008, Barack Obama was elected to do one thing: to not be George W. Bush. The electorate voted against Bush's wars of choice, civil liberties abuses, executive power grabs and government secrecy, all in the name of national security.

Rightly or wrongly, they also blamed Bush for a bad economy. He certainly hadn't done anything to help.

During his campaign, former constitutional law professor Barack Obama promised to end the wars, restore constitutional protections of civil liberties, and run a "transparent" administration. He promised to review every one of Bush's executive orders and overturn any that "trampled on liberty." He promised to close the prison camp at Guantanamo Bay.

For the liberals, he promised to fight against the cozy relationship between multinational corporations and Washington, D.C.

Obama did wind down the wars in Iraq and Afghanistan, but he started several new ones, with results even more disastrous.

Siding with rebels in Libya to overthrow former U.S. adversary-turned-partner Muammar Gadhafi, the Obama administration allowed the country to be taken over by much more radical Islamists. Ditto for Egypt.

Siding with rebels in Syria to overthrow the Bashar al-Assad regime, the administration has inadvertently armed and trained thousands of jihadists who subsequently joined the Islamic State (IS), if there was ever a distinction between the two groups to begin with.

On one occasion alone, over a thousand rebels, carrying U.S.-supplied arms and equipment, defected from the rebellion in Syria and joined IS in Iraq.[2]

Where Bush was accused of misleading Congress to gain its support for the Iraq War, Obama hasn't asked Congress for authorization at all. So much for the constitutional law professor.

Every dollar borrowed to fund these wars is a dollar that can't be lent to a business to expand and create new jobs. It's not just a dollar that is paid to a soldier instead. There's a lot more waste when the government spends money than when private employers spend it. Since 1996, there has been $8.5 trillion in funds sent to the Pentagon *that they can't account for at all.*[3]

At home, Obama hasn't fared much better at not being Bush. Thanks to Edward Snowden, the American public now knows that government spying goes well beyond what they understood was occurring under Bush. Instead of rolling it back, Obama has expanded it.

He built a massive NSA data center in Utah to store phone, e-mail and other data belonging to American citizens, all obtained without probable cause or warrants. The center inspired so much public outrage that a Utah legislator actually introduced a bill to cut off its water supply.[4]

I couldn't make this stuff up.

The prison camp at Guantanamo remains open. Despite his frequent condemnations of the use of torture, his administration continues to employ it.[5]

As for transparency, Erica Werner at the Huffington Post notes the irony that Obama accepted an award for transparency "behind closed doors with no media coverage or public access allowed."[6]

On corporatism, Obama has consistently poured gasoline on the fire. The Dodd-Frank legislation he signed into law allows too-big-to-fail banks to become even bigger and more of a threat if they fail. His forays into "investing into green energy" have been nothing more than typical crony capitalism, ending in disasters like Solyndra.

Then, there's the Affordable Care Act.

Hardcore liberals wanted a government-run, single payer healthcare system. They wanted "Medicare for everyone." What they got was another crony capitalist scheme that showered hundreds of billions on corporate health insurers, made healthcare more expensive for everyone, and may not have decreased the net number of uninsured at all.

"Obamacare" was originally the Republican answer to Hillarycare in the 1990s. Republican governor Mitt Romney implemented a version of it in Massachusetts. Whether they're right or wrong about what they want, Obamacare is nothing like what the hard left elected Obama to give them.

Everyone else likes it even less. 2014 Gallup polls show Americans disapprove of Obamacare by a clear majority.[7]

Heading into the 2014 midterm elections, a majority of Americans, including 59% of those not affiliated with either of the two major parties, disapproved of the job President Obama was doing.[8] Like Bush in 2006, the president was a liability on the campaign trail for his own party, which lost control of the Senate in that election.

Thank goodness the conservatives are different, right? Wrong.

In 2000, George W. Bush campaigned on the usual Republican platitudes of free markets, smaller government and individual liberty. He even harkened back to Old Right values, including "a humble foreign policy." He said that it was not America's job to be the policeman of the world.

How did that work out?

On promoting the free market, Bush and the Republican Congress couldn't have been worse. They only enacted two significant economic policies: the Sarbanes-Oxley Act and the TARP Bailout.

One was a massive increase in regulation and the other an equally massive government subsidy to Wall Street.

On both occasions, Bush evoked one of the most anti-free market presidents in U.S. history. He called Sarbanes-Oxley "the most far-reaching reforms of American business practices since the time of Franklin Delano Roosevelt."[9]

On TARP, Bush claimed he "abandoned free market principles to save the free market," something liberals routinely credit FDR with in making their case for even more regulation.

Bush consistently endorsed the misconception that economic crises are the result of free markets, rather than the government interventions that really caused them. His explanation for the housing crisis was "Wall Street got drunk."

Before the first vote on TARP Americans of all political persuasions bombarded their representatives with angry phone calls, e-mails and demonstrations. Congressmen were visibly scared. They voted it down the first time.

But they eventually passed it, with Bush, Obama, and Republican nominee John McCain all in support. Bush helped cool grassroots opposition with a passionate speech designed to scare the daylights out of us. Enough people believed him to allow Congress to ram it through.

As for "small government," Bush and the Republicans increased federal spending 50% over Clinton's last year in office in just six years. It was $2.7 trillion by 2007. It would top $3 trillion before Bush left office.[10] "Big spending liberal" Bill Clinton only increased it by 25% over all eight years of his presidency.

One might offer 9/11 as an explanation for Bush's failures either to curb spending or to execute a humble foreign policy. After all, a military response to 9/11 was necessary and wars cost money.

That makes a nice story, but it just doesn't jibe with the facts. Of that $2.7 trillion spent in 2007, only $70 billion was spent on the wars in Iraq and Afghanistan *combined*.[11] That leaves $800 billion in increases to account for.

Moreover, the majority of that $70 billion was spent in Iraq, a war virtually everyone acknowledges was unnecessary, unrelated to 9/11 and a mistake. The Iraq war and the very un-humble foreign policy it represented was the single biggest reason Republicans lost Congress in 2006 and the White House in 2008.

Then, there is individual liberty. Bush broke new ground in trashing the Bill of Rights with his warrantless wiretaps, surveillance of financial data and expansions of executive power. Between the Patriot Act and Military Commissions Act of 2006, the Fourth and Fifth Amendments went out the window.

You don't have to be a constitutional scholar to know there's something very wrong with the government eavesdropping on your phone calls without a warrant and being able to arrest and hold you indefinitely without charges or any appeal to a judge.

Didn't we used to make fun of the Soviets for this?

The policies enacted by Bush and the Republicans couldn't contrast more with their rhetoric or the reasons conservative voters say they elect them. It's insane.

We've tried every possible configuration within the two party system. We've given the Republicans control of the White House and Congress. Then, we gave Congress back to the Democrats. After that, we gave the Democrats the White House and Congress. Now, we've given Congress back to the Republicans.

We've tried it all and Washington, D.C. is as broken as ever.

The economy continues to falter. The government tells us unemployment is decreasing, while at the same time acknowledging they don't count people who've given up looking for work.

Does anyone really believe unemployment is really down?

They tell us what they call "inflation" is under control, while at the same time acknowledging they play tricks with those numbers, too.

Does anyone really believe prices haven't gone up?

There are some things Washington doesn't even try to deny. The wars go on. The federal debt continues to increase. The unfunded liabilities of Social Security and Medicare continue to explode, unaddressed. Young people know they won't be getting the benefits. Why should they continue to pay?

Regardless of our politics or what Washington tells us, we all have a sinking feeling that won't seem to go away. Something is wrong with the world. We just don't know what it is.

Often, we're told the representatives we elect aren't "real liberals" or "real conservatives." Grassroots conservatives have even come up with a clever acronym for this phenomenon: "RINO." It stands for "Republican in Name Only." It's meant to describe a Republican who campaigns on conservative rhetoric but acts more like a liberal Democrat when in office.

Both liberals and conservatives believe their representatives don't truly believe in liberal or conservative principles, respectively. If only they could elect genuine liberals or genuine conservatives, the government would get back to representing the people, the economy would revive, and Washington, D.C. would "work."

This book is going to challenge those assertions.

What if the conservatives in Washington *are* the real conservatives? What if they actually do what they say they will, if you listen closely enough? What if conservatism isn't really what most Americans think it is? What if the "RINOs" are the real Republicans?

What if all of the above is true for liberalism as well? What if Nancy Pelosi and Harry Reid are the real liberals?

There are a few basic principles that virtually all Americans still claim to believe in. They are summarized in the preamble to the Declaration of Independence:

"We hold these truths to be self-evident, that all men are created equal, that they are endowed by their Creator with certain unalienable Rights, that among these are Life, Liberty and the pursuit of Happiness, That to secure these rights, Governments are instituted among Men, deriving their just powers from the consent of the governed, That whenever any Form of Government becomes destructive of these ends, it is the Right of the People to alter or to abolish it, and to institute new Government, laying its foundation on such principles and organizing its powers in such form, as to them shall seem most likely to effect their Safety and Happiness."

There are few, if any, Americans who would disavow that short passage. It is so universally accepted that we'll call it the American Creed.

Jefferson had a gift for conveying enormous ideas in very few words. This was one of his finest moments. In those one hundred thirty-four words, he captured all of the elements of the political treatises of his time. It's worthwhile to take a moment and break it down.

First, the Creed talks about what philosophers back then called "the state of nature." The state of nature is the condition man would find himself in if there were no government. Critics sometimes mistake this to mean some ancient time when we all wore fig leaves and ate only what we could find on the ground or club over the head. They misunderstand the term "state of nature" to mean a time before government ever existed anywhere on earth. That's not correct.

The state of nature can occur anywhere and anytime, wherever and whenever there is no effective government to enforce law and order. Think "Lord of the Flies." But it doesn't have to be on a desert island, either. Thomas Hobbes and John Locke observed that all princes existed in a state of nature relative to each other, because there was no government over them.

The Creed says that in the state of nature we are all equal and have certain rights. These rights come from our Creator and are inherent. They aren't granted to us by any government. These rights are also "unalienable," meaning they cannot be taken away. Neither can we surrender them ourselves. Unalienable rights are as much a part of us as our own skins.

The Creed then tells us the purpose of government: to secure these unalienable rights. That's a very limited purpose that necessarily precludes other things some people believe governments are supposed to do. But the Creed is unambiguous. Government's purpose is to secure these rights, period.

The Creed concludes by reminding us that whenever the government becomes "destructive of these ends," meaning it fails to protect *or itself violates* our unalienable rights, we have the right to alter or abolish the government and construct a new one.

Both liberals and conservatives claim their philosophies are the true basis for the American Creed. In the chapters ahead, we're going to examine the foundational conservative and liberal philosophers to try to confirm or deny those claims.

Along the way, we're going to meet some interesting people, like Thomas Hobbes, John Locke, Jean-Jacques Rousseau and others. But don't worry. We're not going to spend hours analyzing the categorical imperative or rubbing our chins and asking "Why am I here?"

We *are* going to revisit what these writers and thinkers said about the nature of man, the purpose of government, and the extent of the government's power and compare their ideas to the American Creed.

In other words, we're not just going to rehash what conservative and liberal politicians have said and done. We're going to try to figure out *why* they said and did those things. We're going to try to figure out how they *think.*

The results are going to surprise you.

Tom Mullen

Chapter Two:

Where Do Conservatives Come From?

"This country is planted thick with laws from coast to coast, Man's laws, not God's, and if you cut them down – and you're just the man to do it – do you really think you could stand upright in the winds that would blow then? Yes, I give the Devil benefit of law, for my own safety's sake!""

- Attributed to Sir Thomas More in *A Man for All Seasons* by Robert Bolt[1]

Conservatives get their name from their desire to "conserve" the socio-political structure as it is. If change must occur, it should be gradual and as undisruptive as possible. Rather than "liberal," the true opposite of conservative is really "radical," as in "radical change." That more than any specific policy is what the conservative fears most.

American conservatives are divided into two groups, as were their British forebears. They generally agree on most things. They share the same vision of the nature of man, the purpose of government, and the extent of the power invested in government. They disagree on the form of government or how that power should be distributed.

We'll call the first group "centralizers," because they seek to centralize government power, both in a national government and in the executive branch. That's something liberals accused George Bush of trying to do with executive orders, signing statements, and other "unilateral" executive policies.

We'll call the second group "constitutionalists," because they seek to divide power between national, state and local governments and between separate branches within those governments. These would be more like "Old Right" conservatives Robert Taft or Barry Goldwater. A resurgence of Old Right conservatism is emerging today out of the Tea Party movement, with its emphasis on constitutional checks and balances.

While these two groups of conservatives have fought some epic internal battles over the course of American history, they have also worked together just as often. As they agree on most things, they tend to close ranks to resist perceived threats to their shared principles.

The literary traditions of British and American conservatism are rich. One could name hundreds of works as important in understanding conservatism. However, there are two men who are very much foundational: Thomas Hobbes and Edmund Burke.

Hobbes plays the larger role in developing the philosophy of conservatism. Living a century before Burke, he develops the tenets of conservatism from "the ground up," articulating conservative ideas that

Burke would echo later. Their chief differences are on the form of government. Hobbes was a centralizer and Burke a constitutionalist.

Conservatives on the nature of man

All conservatives agree on man's nature. In a word, we're bad. Very bad. So bad that life without government is "solitary, poor, nasty, brutish, and short."[2]

Hobbes lays out this view in his massive work, *Leviathan or The Matter, Forme and Power of a Common Wealth Ecclesiasticall and Civil,* generally referred to simply as *Leviathan.*

First, he discusses man's condition in the state of nature:

"Nature hath made men so equal in the faculties of body and mind as that, though there be found one man sometimes manifestly stronger in body or of quicker mind than another, yet when all is reckoned together the difference between man and man is not so considerable as that one man can thereupon claim to himself any benefit to which another may not pretend as well as he."[3]

That sentence was written over three hundred years ago. We're going to be looking at passages like this from time to time to demonstrate just how long some of these ideas have been around. Don't let the "haths" and "thereupons" throw you. We'll provide translations in 21st century English wherever necessary.

In this passage, Hobbes is just saying "all men are created equal," just like in the American Creed. But then he says this:

"From this equality of ability ariseth equality of hope in the attaining of our ends. And therefore, if any two men desire the same thing, which nevertheless they cannot both enjoy, they become enemies, and in the way to their end, which is principally their own conservation, and sometimes their delectation only, endeavor to destroy or subdue one another."[4]

Where the American Creed says that man's natural equality is the source of our rights, Hobbes says it is the source of all human conflict. Talk about a glass half empty kind of guy! It gets worse:

"Hereby it is manifest that during the time men live without a common power to keep them all in awe, they are in that condition which is called war, and such a war as is of every man against every man."[5]

Hobbes actually believes that man's natural state – meaning his condition in the absence of any government (whether twenty thousand years ago or tomorrow) – is a state of war. That's pretty grim, but it is the basis for all conservative thinking. Not only does man need a government, but one powerful enough to "keep him in awe." Otherwise, he is in a de facto state of war with every other man.

This isn't just a 17th century idea. If you've seen the movie *Apocalypse Now*, it conveys the same message. It was based on a book called *Heart of Darkness* by lifelong conservative Joseph Conrad. Conrad's novel was set in colonial Africa, while Francis Ford Coppola resets the story in the Viet Nam War, but the message of both is identical. As the main character, Marlowe, travels farther up the river and into the unsettled interior, he gets farther from the confines of society and government. The farther from these confines he gets, the more savage and insane the people become. The journey ends with Kurtz, who embodies man's true nature when unrestrained by government. Man literally has a "heart of darkness."

Whether you agree or not, both the movie and the book convey the idea brilliantly. Coppola also weaves in the insanity of war as a theme, without losing Conrad's original message.

Burke and the constitutionalists are in lockstep with Hobbes on the nature of man. Russell Kirk, the 20th century intellectual leader of Burkean conservatism, says this in his own introduction to *Leviathan*:

"What must strike the reader with especial force, in this cold and relentless book, is the almost diabolical truth in Hobbes' interpretation of human nature."[6]

He also presents Burke's view of man's nature as indistinguishable from Hobbes':

"Burke knew that just under the skin of modern man stirs the savage, the brute, the demon. Millennia of bitter experience have taught man how to hold his wilder nature in a precarious restraint; that dread knowledge is expressed in myth, ritual, usage, instinct, prejudice."[7]

Now that you're really feeling good about yourself, let's go a bit further. We've established that man is bad and that it's unfortunate that we are all created equal, because it brings out even more badness in us. What about those "inalienable rights?" Are we endowed by our Creator with rights to life, liberty and the pursuit of happiness? Not quite.

"And because the condition of man (as hath been declared in the precedent chapter) is a condition of war of everyone against everyone (in which case everyone is governed by his own reason and there is nothing he can make use of that may not be a help unto him in preserving his life against his enemies), it followeth that in such a condition every man has a right to everything, even to one another's body."[8]

Hobbes takes a completely different approach to the concept of rights than does the American Creed. Where the Creed describes rights as moral principles, Hobbes is more mechanistic. Forget "what ought to be," Hobbes is only concerned with what goes down when the rubber hits the road. And what really goes down is killing, looting, pillaging, cars turned over and burning…You get the picture.

Again, Burke agrees here with Hobbes. He quotes Hobbes directly in *Reflections on the Revolution in France*,

"Government is not made in virtue of natural rights, which may and do exist in total independence of it; and exist in much greater clearness, and in a much greater degree of abstract perfection: but their abstract perfection is their practical defect. *By having a right to everything they want everything.* Government is a contrivance of human wisdom to provide for human wants. Men have a right that these wants should be provided for by this wisdom. Among these wants is to be reckoned the want, out of civil society, of a sufficient restraint upon their passions. Society requires not only that the passions of individuals should be subjected, but that even in the mass and body as well as in the individuals, *the inclinations of men should frequently be thwarted, their will controlled, and their passions brought into subjection.*"[9]

The idea that man has "a right to everything" in the state of nature completely contradicts the American Creed. The Creed assumes rights are negative. They describe what other people *should not* do to you.

For example, the right to life is not the positive right to live under any circumstances. When someone is killed in an earthquake, we feel bad about it, but we do not say his right to life was violated. The right to life is specifically the right *not to be killed* by another human being.

Similarly, the right to liberty is the right not to have someone forcibly interfere with your peaceful actions. You might want to fly. That you can't does not violate your right to liberty. Only violent interference by other people constitutes a violation of your right to liberty.

Implicit in the American Creed is the existence of these rights in the state of nature. They are not endowed by government, but by our Creator. That governments are created "to secure these rights" confirms that they must exist *before* government.

But conservatives don't believe that. They believe that man has a right to everything in the state of nature, even to one another's bodies, meaning there can be no rights to life, liberty or the pursuit of happiness in this state. Since these rights do not exist without government, then the purpose of government must be something other than what the Creed says it is.

Hobbes goes on to say that none of the benefits of civil society are possible in this state, because man's entire life is dominated by the constant fear of violent death. Without a government "to keep them in awe," men cannot acquire property or benefit from the division of labor, because other men will immediately attack them and steal whatever they produce.

He goes so far as to say that death of natural causes is rare in the state of nature. Yikes!

So, as far as the state of nature goes, both Hobbes and Burke reject the tenets of the American Creed, as do the schools of thought they founded within conservatism. Russell Kirk sums up the conservative position on the Creed when discussing John Randolph:

"John Randolph of Roanoke wholly repudiated the common interpretation of the Declaration of Independence, denounced Jefferson as a Pied Piper, and turned his back upon political abstractions to seek security in prescription and in an unbroken vigilance over personal and local rights."[10]

Conservatives on the purpose of government

Burke summed up well what conservatives see as the purpose of government. Government exists to "thwart" man's natural inclinations and to take him out of the state of war and into a state of relative peace.

Burke gets this idea from Hobbes as well, who said that men form government for the purpose of "getting themselves out from that miserable condition of war, which is necessarily consequent (as hath been shown [ch.xiii]) to the natural passion of men, when there is no visible power to keep them in awe, and tie them by fear of punishment to the performance of their covenants and observation of those laws of nature set down in the fourteenth and fifteenth chapters."[11]

This idea that only the awesome power of government can keep our dark nature at bay explains quite a bit about the way conservatives react to the world today. While non-conservatives have a natural instinct to resist what they think is a bad law, even to practice civil disobedience, this scares the living daylights out of conservatives. They believe it's better to follow a bad law until it is changed than to undermine the authority of the government in any way. Once the idea of resisting a law is introduced, we're on our way back to the state of nature, which is a state of war.

It also explains why conservatives generally support law enforcement officers no matter what the circumstances. Rarely will you see conservatives side with an alleged victim of police brutality. Their first instinct is always to side with the police officer. That's because they see the "thin blue line" as more than just functionaries who enforce the law. To conservatives, they are literally all that stands between civilization and the inherent state of war that exists wherever there is an absence of government force.

There's a scene in the classic film *Gone with the Wind* which captures this idea beautifully. As Rhett Butler and Scarlett O'Hara try to escape Atlanta ahead of the Yankees, the retreating Confederate Army momentarily blocks their way. Scarlett remarks, "Dear, I wish they'd hurry," to which Butler replies,

"I wouldn't be in such a hurry to see them go, if I were you, my dear. With them goes the last semblance of law and order."

Before the soldiers are even out of view, a bench is thrown through a shop window and the looting and pillaging begins. It may be a bit of an exaggeration, but the point is made. The minute government force is not present, man reverts to his natural, savage state.

This reasoning also explains conservative support of the war on drugs, even when confronted by its obvious failure. Conservatives see the use of recreational drugs as a departure from the kind of lifestyle that helps ensure an orderly, peaceful society. Like the concept of "gateway drugs," conservatives see any departure from tradition as "gateway behavior" that will lead to other breakdowns of the laws and traditions which protect us from ourselves.

Conservatives on the extent of government power

As Hobbes says repeatedly throughout his treatise, the power of government must keep men "in awe." Since man has no rights in the state of nature, he carries nothing with him into society. He transfers all of his individual authority over to the sovereign power, whose power is absolute and inalienable.

A government of absolute power is incompatible with the idea of "inalienable rights," which conservatives do not believe in. Again, this is not only a conservative tenet from hundreds of years ago. Kirk confirms this as late as the 1950s:

"And natural rights do not exist independent of circumstances; what may be a right on one occasion and for one man, may be unjust folly for another man at a different time. Prudence is the test of actual right. Society may deny men prerogatives because they are unfit to exercise them."[12]

It's important to remember the difference between the powers vested in a government and the particular form government takes. Hobbes and Burke both believe the government should have absolute and inalienable power, but differ on how that power is distributed throughout the government.

This is very relevant to 21st century America. Today, Americans typically think of "democracy" as the type of government that provides freedom, while dictatorships or monarchies provide less freedom or no freedom at all.

However, it is not the *form* of government that determines the freedom of the people, but the *power* that government is allowed to wield. A dictator could theoretically provide more freedom than a democracy, if the dictator's powers were limited and the democracy's powers were not.

Hobbes takes pains to remind us of this distinction throughout Leviathan. When he speaks of the sovereign power, he often includes the parenthetical qualification "whether a monarch or an assembly."

The inalienability of government power also contradicts the American Creed. Hobbes argues that once a commonwealth is formed and sovereign power invested in the government, the subjects can never change the form of that government. This completely contradicts the Creed's assertion that the people have the right to alter or abolish their government and replace it with another.

Burke for the most part agrees in principle, if not in degree. He bases his criticism of the French Revolution on the Hobbesian idea that once the social contract made, it binds not only the people who made it, but all of their descendants. In Burke's own words,

"The law by which this royal family is specifically destined to succession, is the act of the 12th and 13th of King William. The terms of this act bind 'us and our *heirs*, and our *posterity*, to them, their *heirs*, and their *posterity*,' being Protestants, to the end of time, in the same words as the declaration of right had bound us to the heirs of King William and Queen Mary."[13]

For Burke, the only circumstances under which the people are ever justified in dissolving the government and forming a new one are those where the king has committed such heinous acts against the people that he has fundamentally violated the social contract made between the monarchy and the people's ancestors. Outside of that, the people are permanently bound by the contract made by their ancestors.

This would seem to contradict Burke's support of the American Revolution, but it does not. Burke's support of the Americans was based upon his opinion that the sovereign power *had* broken the social contract. He sees the attempt by Parliament to impose new taxes on the colonies and legislate in areas they hadn't before as "innovations," or breaks with the established contract between people and sovereign.

Burke's position on the revolution is completely consistent with conservatism and explains one reason the American Revolution was successful: both conservatives and their opponents found common ground to unite in opposition to the mother country. Conservatives supported the revolution based on Burke's argument. Non-conservatives supported the revolution for their own reasons.

The assumption that the subjects of a commonwealth must invest absolute and inalienable power in the government leads Hobbes to conclusions that would seem shocking to most modern Americans. Hobbes asserts that the sovereign is above the law and cannot be punished by his subjects.

The sovereign must even determine what teachings, both secular and religious, are proper for the people to have access to, as the sovereign must be "judge of what opinions and doctrines are averse, and what conducing, to peace."[14]

This explains the importance of religion in politics for conservatives. For Hobbes, people must have the proper religious beliefs or they will be tempted to undermine the sovereign power, which must never be challenged. Therefore, the head of state should also be the highest religious authority, as the King of England was head of the Church of England.

Burke also believed that a state religion should be a government institution. As Kirk puts it,

"To inculcate this veneration among men, to consecrate public office, Burke believed that the church must be interwoven with the fabric of the nation…'Religion is so far, in my opinion, from being out of the province of a Christian magistrate,' Burke wrote, 'that it is, and it ought to be, not only his care, but the principal thing in his care; and its object the supreme good, the ultimate end and object of man himself.'"[15]

Both Burke and Kirk go so far as to say that the state itself *is ordained by God* to restrain the evil impulses of mankind. Even public policy they oppose vehemently is chalked up to the will of God if it overcomes their opposition and becomes firmly established legal tradition.

Opponents of conservatism today tend to see conservatives as seeking to impose their religious beliefs on other people out of petty tyranny. Whether you agree with Hobbes and Burke or not, examining their positions should at least inspire a little sympathy for conservatives on this point. They don't promote the influence of religion in government just to impose their beliefs on other people. They truly believe society will break down without it.

Since the rights to life and liberty are not inalienable and carried into society, conservatives see them as privileges granted by the government. The government determines the bounds of liberty within society.

Rick Santorum was widely criticized for expressing this basic conservative principle during a 2012 Republican primary debate while responding to fellow candidate Ron Paul. Immediately afterwards, Santorum's earlier comments in a 2005 NPR interview were all over the media:

"One of the criticisms I make is to what I refer to as more of a Libertarianish right. They have this idea that people should be left alone, be able to do whatever they want to do, government should keep our taxes down and keep our regulations low, that we shouldn't get involved in the bedroom, we shouldn't get involved in cultural issues. That is not how traditional conservatives view the world. There is no such society that I am aware of, where we've had radical individualism and that it succeeds as a culture."[16]

Libertarians went apoplectic at this statement. David Boaz of the Cato Institute told Judge Andrew Napolitano the he didn't "know of any other politician, other than Rick Santorum and Hillary Clinton, who have directly attacked the idea of the pursuit of happiness. It's in the Declaration. It's the fundamental idea of America."[17]

Boaz was wrong about there not being other politicians who agree with Santorum. Whether you agree with him or not, Santorum's is right about one thing. Traditional conservatives do not see the world the way libertarians do. In fact, they don't really believe there are inalienable rights, including to the pursuit of happiness. They may say they do, but the when it comes to applying that principle to policy, they consistently react as Santorum did here.

That government defines the amount of liberty people can enjoy is another old conservative idea. As Hobbes argues,

"Seventhly, is annexed to the sovereignty the whole power of prescribing the rules whereby every man may know what goods he many enjoy, and what actions he may do, without being molested by any of his fellow-subjects; and this is it men call propriety."[18]

In addition to liberty, Hobbes says the government also determines what right its constituents have to the ownership of property. This is also a departure from the Creed, as property rights are implicit in the pursuit of happiness. We'll see in a later chapter that the natural right to acquire property and dispose of it as you wish is inextricably tied to the American Creed. It's essential to pursuing happiness in the real world.

That's not to say that happiness is solely determined by the accumulation of material wealth. Far from it. But the freedom to acquire property and dispose of it as one sees fit is necessary to be able to pursue one's dreams, whether they are material, intellectual or spiritual. If you want to quit working and devote the rest of your life to study or prayer, you're going to need material means to keep yourself alive in order to do it. That's not being overly materialistic, just realistic.

Conservatives certainly defend private property rights, but not as a natural right. Rather, they are privileges bestowed by the government to individuals for the betterment of society as a whole, just like liberty. This has serious implications for their economic policy.

Kirk argues that Burke and the constitutional conservatives depart from Hobbes in that they rely not only on government power, but also on "the old motives to integrity, the old religious disciplines, and all those tender elements of *free and local association*"[19] to restrain man's passions [emphasis added].

For Burke, our rights are the result of these longstanding traditions, rather than merely what liberty and property the government allows us to enjoy. He calls these "prescriptive rights," meaning rights based upon longstanding custom. Kirk constantly refers back to these throughout his *Conservative Mind* as essential to preserving a free society.

His characterization of these traditions as free associations might lead one to believe that Burkeans believe rights are more than just government-granted privileges.

But this is disingenuous. The institutions Kirk refers to may be local, but they are hardly free. One cannot refer to a state religion with a tax subsidized clergy and legally mandated participation as a "free association" without grossly abusing the English language.

Whether religion, inheritance laws, local regulation of tradesman or a dozen other institutions, both Kirk's and Burke's objections to "destruction" of longstanding customs amount to resistance to *removing legal mandates and subsidies*. Put bluntly, these institutions only became longstanding because people were forced to continue them by the government, whether local or central. How is this different from Hobbes?

For example, Kirk decries "the levelling agrarian republicanism of which Jefferson's was the chief representative, zealous to abolish entail, primogeniture, church establishments, and all the vestiges of aristocracy…"[20]

The word "levelling" is misleading, as it suggests positive government redistribution of wealth, which Jefferson consistently denounced. Kirk conflates removing existing government power with granting it new power. This is by no means the only occasion.

Abolishing primogeniture actually *enhanced* property rights. Primogeniture required fathers to bequeath all of their estates to their first born sons, regardless of the father's wishes. Abolishing primogeniture didn't prohibit the father bequeathing to the first born son; it merely gave the father *the freedom to do otherwise if he wished*. The right to dispose of one's property as one sees fit is an essential element of owning property at all.

Similarly, Jefferson didn't attempt to abolish churches. He merely proposed that churches no longer be subsidized. Before the revolution, Virginia subsidized the Anglican Church, but not others. After abolition of the subsidy, Virginians were still able to and still did attend church, including the Anglican Church. They were simply no longer *forced* to subsidize the sovereign's church.

Conservatives are so reluctant to change established legal traditions that they typically defend institutions they previously opposed if they're around long enough. When the New Deal was first proposed, conservatives passionately opposed it as destroying the foundation of American society. They were correct that it was a fundamental, constitutional change.

Fifty years later, Ronald Reagan raised taxes to allow Social Security to continue, saying the bill "demonstrates for all time our nation's ironclad commitment to Social Security."

During the 2012 elections, "fiscal hawk" Paul Ryan excoriated President Obama because his Affordable Care Act threatened the stability of Social Security and Medicare.

Libertarian author Tom Woods expresses frustration with this tendency, writing "Someday, Conservatives Will Defend Obamacare."

"What were once fought tooth and nail as wealth redistribution and obvious violations of the Constitution are now 'conservative New Deal principles.' The word 'entitlement' is used favorably as well. Defending such things has become conservative, now that enough time has passed.

We just want to administer the programs of liberalism more efficiently, and call it conservatism."[21]

The reasoning here isn't mysterious. When the New Deal was first proposed by FDR, it was a break with established legal tradition. It was therefore a threat to societal order, for all of the reasons previously stated. Now that it has been in place for decades, *conservatives view it as the established legal tradition* and vehemently defend it.

This is all consistent with Hobbes' original premise that to challenge the sovereign power, regardless of how objectionably it is wielded, is to endanger all of civil society. It is better to suffer under bad laws than to risk civil war or chaos by changing them.

There really is no disagreement between Hobbesian centralizers and Burkean constitutionalists on the extent of the powers of government. Conservatives from Hobbes to Burke to Rick Santorum believe government power should regulate all areas of life. It is on how this power should be organized and distributed that conservatives are divided.

Conservatives on the form of government

For Hobbes and the centralizers, all power is invested in a sovereign and is indivisible. Hobbes is against any mixed form of government because it de facto results in a separation of powers. He acknowledges the many dangers of putting absolute power into the hands of one man, but argues that any government by an assembly, either elected or aristocratic, suffers from the same "inconveniences" while offering none of the security a monarchy can provide. He acknowledges that indivisible sovereign power can be invested in an assembly, but believes absolute monarchy is preferable.

"Fifthly, that in monarchy there is this inconvenience: that any subject, by the power of one man, for the enriching of a favourite or flatterer, may be deprived of all he possesseth; which I confess is a great and inevitable inconvenience. But the same may as well happen where the sovereign power is in an assembly; for their power is the same, and they are as subject to evil counsel, and to be seduced by orators, as a monarch by flatterers; and becoming one another's flatterers, serve one another's covetousness and ambition by turns."[22]

Hobbes would have been completely against the U.S. Constitution, particularly the idea that the different branches of government should retain their own independent powers and check each other. He didn't necessarily oppose the existence of the British Parliament, as long as it rubber stamped the wishes of the king. But the sovereign power should never be divided. That only weakens it and increases the danger of returning to the state of nature or civil war.

This reasoning also informs Hobbes' assertion that the secular and ecclesiastical authority must be united. As the scriptures are open to interpretation, it is up to the sovereign to decide which interpretations will be accepted by his subjects. The subjects must be educated according to the wishes of the sovereign and in such a way that they will not question the sovereign power nor the form of government they live under. Therefore, the sovereign dictates the form and content of education and even appoints the pastors of churches.

God forbid any subject of the sovereign entertain a religious idea that even questions the dictates of the monarch. From any individual right of conscience comes dissolution of the sovereign power, civil war, and eventual decline into the miserable state of nature. It is far better for the monarch to tell people what to believe, regardless of their opinions.

Hobbes conscientiously practices what he preaches in this respect. For, although he spends over 250 pages undertaking the monumental task of interpreting all of the Christian bible, he says he would be willing to change his interpretation if his monarch so ordered him!

Burke and the constitutionalists mostly agree with Hobbes on the marriage between religious and political power; they just don't believe it should be centralized. When Burkean constitutional conservative John Adams drafted the first Massachusetts constitution, it allowed the legislature to pass laws making religious instruction mandatory. However, it stipulated that the local towns and parishes retained the right of electing the teachers. It read,

"To promote their happiness and to secure the good order and preservation of their government, the people of this commonwealth have a right to invest their legislature with power to authorize and require, and the legislature shall, from time to time, authorize and require, the several towns, parishes, precincts, and other bodies-politic or religious societies to make suitable provision, at their own expense, for the institution of the public worship of God and for the support and maintenance of public Protestant teachers of piety, religion, and morality in all cases where such provision shall not be made voluntarily.

And the people of this commonwealth have also a right to, and do, invest their legislature with authority to enjoin upon all the subject an attendance upon the instructions of the public teachers aforesaid, at stated times and seasons, if there be any on whose instructions they can conscientiously and conveniently attend.

Provided, notwithstanding, That the several towns, parishes, precincts, and other bodies-politic, or religious societies, shall at all times have the exclusive right and electing their public teachers and of contracting with them for their support and maintenance."[23]

This same argument continues today regarding both religion and education. Hobbesian centralizers supported George Bush's initiatives to subsidize (and thereby control) "faith-based organizations" to perform some government social services and "No Child Left Behind" to subsidize (and thereby control) public education.

Constitutional conservatives don't necessarily believe public money shouldn't be spent on either of these functions, but they believe it should be local or state governments who do the subsidizing and controlling, not the federal government.

This is really the way Burke and the constitutionalists think on all issues. Their one substantive departure from Hobbes is their unwillingness to centralize all power in one place. Both Hobbes and Burke recognized the potential for abuse, but Hobbes said the abuses of an absolute monarch were worth the price to ensure that the government remained powerful enough to do what it has to do.

Burke and the conservatives in his tradition disagree. They see the king or the legislature as made up of the same fallen creatures that make up the assembly. Dividing the power of government between executive and legislature and federal, state and local governments provides powers to keep the politicians "in awe" and ensure *their* dark natures are not allowed to roam free and create havoc.

But even though the constitutionalists want power divided, it still extends to all areas of life. If the federal government isn't going to regulate a particular area, they want the state government to regulate it. If not the state government, then the municipal. Or the town. Or your local school board. Nothing remains unregulated. The country remains "planted thick with laws."

Conservative economic policy

Today, conservatives constantly profess their belief in free markets, but that doesn't jibe with any of the policy they enact. It may surprise self-identified conservative voters, but conservative politicians have traditionally been the *opponents* of free markets throughout British and American history. We'll get to that in a later chapter.

Conservatives do vigorously defend private property, but for different reasons than true free market proponents. While free markets place power with the individual, both Hobbesian and Burkean conservatives are more concerned with the health of the collective.

If you listen closely, you'll hear this when conservatives talk about economic issues. They consistently promote policies that they say will "build a strong economy" or "promote economic growth." Their arguments are based upon what is best for what Hobbes calls "the commonwealth." Rarely will you hear traditional conservatives promoting an economic policy based upon the property rights of the individual. Their concern is what will make the commonwealth strong as a whole. The collective must remain strong to keep the nature of man at bay.

Kirk continually laments that individualism is destroying society. That's an old conservative idea, too. He writes,

"Burke dreaded a consuming individualism; habit and prejudice induce that conformity without which society cannot endure."[24]

Kirk also looks negatively in general on the industrial revolution. While recognizing its inevitability, he sees is as destroying the old foundations of society where landed aristocrats governed counties and each member of society lived out their lives at the same social level. He repeatedly criticizes self-made men as not being as valuable to society as the old aristocrats.

While Hobbes did not develop his economic ideas extensively, his philosophy forms the basis for mercantilism.

Mercantilism proceeds from the idea that independent nations are all economic rivals, economically mirroring the political state of war Hobbes assumed they exist in. Seeing all economic activity as a "zero sum game," whereby any gain by one economic actor must necessarily come at the expense of another, the mercantilist nation seeks to maintain a positive trade balance, especially concerning the inflows and outflows of gold.

The specific policies of mercantilism include subsidies to favored domestic corporations, protective tariffs and regulations, and other government interventions into the marketplace that tend to protect established firms from new competition.

These policies all help support a wealthy class of aristocrats at the expense of the rest of society. The entrenched elite are both dependent upon government privilege and reciprocally loyal to the sovereign power.

This is the foundation for what we today call "crony capitalism," or "corporatism." Capital is privately owned and commerce is competitive, but heavily regulated. Regulations under the pretense of public safety or protectionism create barriers to entry into the market. This tends to limit the amount of new competition established corporations face at any given time. Exxon may compete with BP or Shell, but not the thousands of other potential competitors it would face if free entry into the market were permitted.

So, when liberals complain about conservatives "supporting the 1% at the expense of the 99%," they aren't completely wrong. In fact, an essential component of conservative theory is the need for an aristocracy.

Even centralist Hobbes wanted his absolute monarch to have the power 'to confer honors and titles." The existence of an elite class of "betters" helps maintain stability and keeps the passions of the mob at bay.

Kirk writes extensively on the need for an aristocracy. He also recognizes this as an essential part of Burke's constitutional worldview:

"Physical and moral anarchy is prevented by general acquiescence in social distinctions of duty and privilege. If a natural aristocracy is not recognized among men, the sycophant and the brute exercise its abandoned functions in the name of a faceless "people."[25]

The mercantilist economy is completely consistent with this. It establishes controlled competition, with the main economic players familiar and their behavior predictable. During the classical mercantilist period, kings would simply grant a monopoly to certain companies for certain products, as George III did for the East India Tea Company.

In today's economy, regulation, subsidies and other government privileges to otherwise privately held firms accomplishes the same goal. There may not be one oil company or media company, but there are a small, comfortable number, both constrained by and dependent upon the government to maintain their position. This protects society from the dramatic change or "creative destruction" that results from laissez faire markets.

Conservatives recognize the need for a market economy with some competition, but they want to control outcomes to some degree so they are not too disruptive to the existing order. Their fear of radical change constantly motivates them to *regulate* in the original sense of the word, meaning "keep regular."

That's why conservatives rarely try to repeal regulations once in power. Instead, they talk about "more sensible regulation." But when confronted with economic crises, virtually always caused by previous government interventions, conservatives consistently respond with more regulation.

That didn't start with George Bush and Sarbanes-Oxley. Remember, it was Richard Nixon who created the Environmental Protection Agency (EPA) by executive fiat. He didn't even ask Congress. He also instituted wage and price controls by executive order. Nixon was a classic Hobbesian in terms of how he achieved those ends, but regulation in general is a bedrock conservative principle.

Looking even farther back, Kirk laments the failure of conservatives to regulate with protectionist policies for English farmers. He sees the industrial revolution as a negative.

"Britain became the most thoroughly industrialized country of the world, perilously overpopulated, saddeningly decayed in taste and beauty; more and more, the national tone was set by the Black Country and the swollen seaports, rather than by the rural parishes and tight little towns that had nourished English political stability, English literature, and English charm."[26]

This is just more application of the central conservative theory. The government must control inheritance, commerce and even religious life to preserve the status quo, lest "innovation" threaten to break down these safeguards against man's savage nature. Burke and Kirk aren't opposing legal prohibitions against longstanding voluntary institutions, because no one was suggesting them. They opposed the removal of legal mandates *forcing* people to participate.

Economically, Kirk suggests that intangibles like "national tone" and "English charm" are essential enough to force English citizens to pay higher prices for food, rather than have access to less expensive imports. He views England naturally moving toward its comparative advantage in manufacturing over farming, the result of the free choices of English market players, as regrettable.

Better that the awesome power of the government was employed to override all of these choices to maintain longstanding custom, despite the hardship in England and devastation in Ireland wrought by protectionism.

Along with subsidies to domestic corporations and high tariffs to protect them from foreign competition, the mercantilist system usually depends upon a central bank to supply the needed liquidity when real savings are not to be found.

This "inflation" of the currency really redistributes wealth from society in general to whomever receives the loans. Again, liberals would say it redistributes wealth from the 99% to the 1%. They're right; it does.

But they're wrong to characterize this as a failure of free markets. Central banking is another departure from the free market that conservatives believe makes the collective stronger, by "creating jobs" or "stimulating economic growth."

In fairness, central banking is more a Hobbesian centralist conservative institution than Burkean constitutionalist. Many Burkean constitutionalists, such as Barry Goldwater in the 1960's or Rand Paul today are sharply critical of the Federal Reserve and its inflationary policies.

In conclusion, conservative economic theory grows naturally out of their general theory of the nature of man and the purpose of government. Rather than peaceful trade to mutual benefit, conservatives see the economy as a war, with winners and losers. They want to allow enough freedom for competition, but they also want to make sure the right people win.

The strength of the society as a whole trumps any individual rights to liberty or property, because it is that collective strength which protects us all from ourselves.

Conservative foreign policy

Most of the enlightenment philosophers viewed foreign policy similarly in one regard. They all viewed the relationship of nations to each other as analogous to the relationships between individuals within society. Thus, all separate political entities exist in a state of nature with each other.

One shouldn't be surprised by what Hobbes says about the relationship of the various nations to each other. As they are in a state of nature, they are therefore in a de facto state of war.

"For as amongst masterless men, there is perpetual war of every man against his neighbor, no inheritance to transmit to the son nor to expect from the father, no propriety of goods or lands, no security, but a full and absolute liberty in every particular man, so in states and commonwealths not dependent on one another every commonwealth (not every man) has an absolute liberty to do what it shall judge (that is to say, what that man or assembly that representeth it shall judge) most conducing to their benefit. But withal, they live in the conditions of a perpetual war and upon the confines of battle, with their frontiers armed and cannons planted against their neighbours round about."[27]

Hobbes does not lay out a detailed foreign policy, but it isn't difficult to infer what kind of foreign policy naturally follows. As all nations exist in a de facto state of war with each other, no nation is safe unless one dominates all the rest, becoming the equivalent among nations of the absolute monarch within the commonwealth.

Along with the mercantilist idea that new markets for a nation's goods can be "opened" militarily, the Hobbesian view of the natural relationship between nations is the primary motivation for empire.

You can hear Hobbes every day in neoconservative rhetoric about the dangers to national security posed by instability in third world countries thousands of miles away. When George Bush said we had to "fight them over there so we won't have to fight them over here," he was being perfectly consistent with this longstanding Hobbesian view of the world. It also inspired the Korean and Viet Nam wars. The so-called "domino theory" was deeply rooted in Hobbesian conservatism.

During the 2012 presidential primaries, Ron Paul suggested that the U.S. should not only withdraw from the Middle East, but bring its troops home from Japan, Korea and Germany. His Republican opponents responded by calling his foreign policy ideas "dangerous."

Rationally, it's hard to substantiate any danger to U.S. citizens from removing U.S. troops from Germany, seventy years after the end of WWII and over twenty years after the fall of the Soviet Union. But it's consistent with the Hobbesian view that all nations are in a state of war with one another, absent domination by one of them. Those troops are needed everywhere to keep other nations "in awe."

From this comes the argument for "American exceptionalism," the idea that the United States as the lone superpower should play the role, if not of world sovereign, at least of world policeman.

While its proponents are called "neoconservatives," there is really nothing new about them or this idea. The British thought in much the same way in expanding their empire, as did early American centralizers like Alexander Hamilton who sought to copy the British Empire in America.

Hobbes invests the sovereign "the right of making war and peace with other nations and commonwealths, that is to say, of judging when it is for the public good."[28] As the sovereign for Hobbes is preferably a monarch, he is empowering one man to take the nation to war. American centralizers seek to invest this power in the president, while constitutionalists point to Congress' sole authority in declaring war.

Burkean conservative Robert Taft's vote against NATO was based partially on his objection to investing the president with the power to take the United States to war:

43

"Under the Monroe Doctrine we could change our policy at any time. We could judge whether perhaps one of the countries had given cause for the attack. Only Congress could declare a war in pursuance of the doctrine. Under the new pact the President can take us into war without Congress."[29]

Constitutional conservatives are also more reluctant to go to war in general. They may not reject the Hobbesian view of the relationship between nations out of hand, but their aversion to centralization of power within the commonwealth translates to a reluctance to expand the commonwealth's authority across national borders.

American constitutional conservatives have traditionally opposed wars, especially in the 20th century when Democratic administrations sought to commit the United States to war for high ideals like "making the world safe for democracy," rather than for some tangible and compelling national interest. Called "isolationists" by their opponents, constitutional conservatives opposed entry into WWI, WWII, the Korean War and the Viet Nam War.

However, they do not object to military interventionism on principle. Burke himself was a supporter of the British Empire. He just objected to the way it was administered at certain times and places, particularly in India.

Similarly today, constitutional conservatives like Rand Paul do not object to U.S. military interventions on principle, but are more reluctant to resort to them and insist they are conducted constitutionally, with a declaration of war by Congress.

Conclusion

The conservative philosophy is inconsistent with the American Creed. Both Hobbesian centralizers and Burkean constitutionalists reject the Creed's assertions that all men are created equal and endowed with inalienable rights. They believe that in the state of nature man has no rights and exists in a perpetual state of war.

Based on this assumption, they do not agree that governments are instituted to secure these rights. Instead, they believe the purpose of government is to restrain man's natural, savage instincts. They believe that liberty and property are privileges bestowed by government, not natural rights which government is tasked with protecting.

Finally, they do not believe the Creed's assertion that it is the right of the people to alter or abolish the government if it fails to protect or violate the rights of the people. Conservatives believe the social contract can be broken only in the case of extreme violations by the sovereign power.

Based on their rejection of the American Creed, conservatives generally support a mercantilist or controlled private property economy over the laissez faire free markets implicit in the Creed. Their foreign policy also departs from the non-aggressive policy implicit in the Creed, although centralist and constitutional conservatives disagree on how and why the nation should go to war.

Obviously, we haven't found the source of the American Creed anywhere within conservatism, neither in its philosophical traditions nor in the application of its principles by politicians. Are the liberals closer to the principles of the Creed?

We'll examine the philosophical basis for liberalism in the next chapter.

Chapter Three:

Where Do Liberals Come From?

"An old English judge once said: "Necessitous men are not free men." Liberty requires opportunity to make a living - a living decent according to the standard of the time, a living which gives man not only enough to live by, but something to live for. "

– Franklin Delano Roosevelt. (1936)[1]

Before determining where they come from, we must first define who liberals are. At one time, the word "liberal" meant a laissez faire approach to economic issues, limited government and maximum individual liberty. That is still roughly how liberal is defined in many European countries. American liberals seem to believe exactly the opposite.

For that reason, many on the left have found it more fashionable to call themselves "progressives," although that term is troublesome as well.

The American progressive movement began around the turn of the 20th century, founded by both conservatives *and* liberals. The first "progressive president" was Teddy Roosevelt, a Republican.

Writing for the Huffington Post, David Sirota attempts to sort it out:

"It seems to me that traditional 'liberals' in our current parlance are those who focus on using taxpayer money to help better society. A "progressive" are those who focus on using government power to make large institutions play by a set of rules.

To put it in more concrete terms - a liberal solution to some of our current problems with high energy costs would be to increase funding for programs like the Low Income Home Energy Assistance Program (LIHEAP). A more 'progressive' solution would be to increase LIHEAP but also crack down on price gouging and pass laws better-regulating the oil industry's profiteering and market manipulation tactics."[2]

For Sirota, the liberal philosophy is limited to government wealth redistribution, while progressivism adds more aggressive regulation. Whether the regulatory component was really missing from 20th century liberalism is debatable, but we'll see in a later chapter that the distinction has some merit.

Regardless, the overwhelming majority of Americans tend to use the word "liberal" to describe supporters of both regulation and redistribution, all of whom tend to vote for the Democratic Party in American elections. As "progressive" is troublesome in that it overlaps with conservatism in some respects, we will do likewise.

Liberals in 21st century America believe the government has a role to both regulate human behavior and redistribute wealth in order to achieve a more "socially just" and equitable society. Liberals are suspicious of laissez faire capitalism due to their belief that it results in too much of society's wealth concentrated in a small percentage of the population, as well as a disregard for the environment.

Liberals have been fiercely anti-war or have supported an aggressive foreign policy, depending upon the reasons for the war and, like conservatives, whether it was started by a Republican or a Democrat.

Like conservatives, liberals claim to be the true standard bearers of the American Creed, particularly that all men are created equal. They view themselves as champions of the middle class and poor, protecting the little guy from exploitation by powerful, "moneyed interests." They are also champions of the "public good," including protecting a clean, safe environment for future generations.

Their critics label them socialists, claiming their true philosophical inspiration comes from Karl Marx. Marx's influence on modern liberalism is undeniable, but it would be dishonest to describe all liberals as Marxist. Most haven't openly advocated for the government to seize the means of production or eliminate private property.

Just like conservatism, liberalism consist of two subgroups who generally agree on the nature of man, his condition in the state of nature, the purpose of government and the extent of its power.

Also like conservatives, the two liberal subgroups disagree on the form the government should take. The first group believes the government should be a pure democracy that allows private property, but regulates and redistributes it. We'll call them democrats (not to be confused with the Democratic Party). These trace their modern roots back to Jean-Jacques Rousseau.

The second group also believes in pure democracy, but that private property should be prohibited and government should own the means of production. These are the socialists. Their modern philosophical roots can be found in the writings of Karl Marx.

Both the democratic and socialist philosophies have its roots in antiquity. If Aristotle is the classical conservative, Plato is the classical liberal, whose ideas still influence liberals today. But it was Rousseau and Marx who laid the modern foundations for liberalism.

Just as Hobbes built the more extensive philosophical theory of conservatism, so did Rousseau for liberalism. Marx is derivative of Rousseau and is more purely focused on economics, although he does make many observations on socio-political theory.

We'll begin with those elements of society that both democrats and socialists agree on.

Rousseau on the nature of man

Rousseau begins his examination of the state of nature by drawing an important distinction. For him, there is a fundamental difference between men in the state of nature *before* the dawn of societies and men in the state of nature *after* they have been exposed to society, particularly the division of labor.

Remember, "state of nature" means the absence of government, not society. There can be an association of individuals who voluntarily cooperate with each other that constitutes a society without there being a government.

Rousseau first seeks to examine the former state of man, without society or government, which he refers to as "savage man."

Hobbes' first observation was that all men are born in a state of equality. Hobbes recognized that one man might be stronger than another or smarter than another, but that the differences did not result in any one man having a natural right to exercise power over another.

In his **Discourses on the Origin of Inequality**, Rousseau makes similar observations, distinguishing between absolute equality and political equality.

Neither Hobbes, Rousseau nor Locke asserted that man is equal in strength, intelligence, or other abilities, but they all believed men in their natural state are equal in terms of any right to exert power over one another.

For Rousseau, equality is the central theme.

"I conceive that there are two kinds of inequality among the human species; one, which I call natural or physical, because it is established by nature, and consists in a difference of age, health, bodily strength, and the qualities of the mind or of the soul: and another, which may be called moral or political inequality, because it depends on a kind of convention, and is established, or at least authorised by the consent of men. This latter consists of the different privileges, which some men enjoy to the prejudice of others; such as that of being more rich, more honoured, more powerful or even in a position to exact obedience."[3]

Of the latter inequality, Rousseau concludes that it does not exist in nature, but is a "convention" invented by men. Thus, he implies man's natural political equality indirectly. He is more explicit in recognizing man's "natural equality" in his *Discourse on Political Economy*. While men naturally have different abilities, they are for all intents and purposes equal in the state of nature.

Unlike Hobbes, Rousseau does not conclude that their equality puts men in a state of war against each other. Instead, Rousseau sees his "savage man" in a state of ignorant innocence, much like Adam and Eve in Genesis. He is governed primarily by his passions, which are few, moderate, and do not include the competitive passions that he develops later. Savage man only develops his reason so far as it is necessary to protect him from predators and to fulfill his basic needs.

"Let us conclude then that man in a state of nature, wandering up and down the forests, without industry, without speech, and without home, an equal stranger to war and to all ties, neither standing in need of his fellow-creatures nor having any desire to hurt them, and perhaps even not distinguishing them one from another; let us conclude that, being self-sufficient and subject to so few passions, he could have no feelings or knowledge but such as befitted his situation; that he felt only his actual necessities, and disregarded everything he did not think himself immediately concerned to notice, and that his understanding made no greater progress than his vanity. If by accident he made any discovery, he was the less able to communicate it to others, as he did not know even his own children. Every art would necessarily perish with its inventor, where there was no kind of education among men, and generations succeeded generations without the least advance; when, all setting out from the same point, centuries must have elapsed in the barbarism of the first ages; when the race was already old, and man remained a child."[4]

You can already see the seeds of bitter conflict between liberals and conservatives. Conservatives see man as a natural devil. Liberals see him as, if not an angel, at least an innocent.

Both view man in nature as primarily governed by his passions, but for Rousseau they are few and limited and not the source of conflict. He sees his savage man as solely concerned with self-preservation, but does not conclude that this leads him into direct conflict with others concerned with their own.

Rousseau also asserts that there is no "industry" in the state of nature, and that man does not stand "in need of his fellow creatures." In other words, Rousseau agrees with Hobbes that there is no division of labor or benefits of complex society in the "savage stage" of the state of nature. For Hobbes this is a defect, for Rousseau, a boon.

Rousseau on natural rights

Rousseau also observes that man in nature is in a state of absolute liberty. However, he disagrees that this means man's actions have no bounds beyond their self-preservation, resulting in perpetual war. He calls out Hobbes explicitly on this point:

"There is another principle which has escaped Hobbes; which, having been bestowed on mankind, to moderate, on certain occasions, the impetuosity of egoism, or, before its birth, the desire of self-preservation, tempers the ardour with which he pursues his own welfare, by an innate repugnance at seeing a fellow-creature suffer.[3] I think I need not fear contradiction in holding man to be possessed of the only natural virtue, which could not be denied him by the most violent detractor of human virtue. I am speaking of compassion, which is a disposition suitable to creatures so weak and subject to so many evils as we certainly are: by so much the more universal and useful to mankind, as it comes before any kind of reflection; and at the same time so natural, that the very brutes themselves sometimes give evident proofs of it."[5]

Rousseau goes on to say that it is pity for the suffering of his fellow creatures that places a limit upon the natural liberty of man in the state of nature. In stark contrast to Hobbes, Rousseau argues that man's passion is what keeps him out of the state of war, specifically his compassion for his fellow man. Rousseau goes on to replace Hobbes' fundamental law of nature with his own.

"… It is this which, instead of inculcating that sublime maxim of rational justice. *Do to others as you would have them do unto you*, inspires all men with that other maxim of natural goodness, much less perfect indeed, but perhaps more useful; *Do good to yourself with as little evil as possible to others*. In a word, it is rather in this natural feeling than in any subtle arguments that we must look for the cause of that repugnance, which every man would experience in doing evil, even independently of the maxims of education. Although it might belong to Socrates and other minds of the like craft to acquire virtue by reason, the human race would long since have ceased to be, had its preservation depended only on the reasonings of the individuals composing it."[6]

Rousseau views compassion or pity as so important an emotion that he actually credits it with the survival of the species, being the force in nature that keeps man out of the state of war.

One can see in these passages the philosophical basis for the "bleeding heart liberal." In less pejorative terms, it forms the basis for the liberal principle that compassion for one's fellow man, rather than solely reason, should play a role in determining public policy.

If you're a conservative, how many times have you been called "heartless" by liberals if you oppose a social program? That's nothing new. It goes back centuries.

This idea resonated in the French Revolution, which replaced the American "life, liberty and the pursuit of happiness" with "liberty, equality, *fraternity*."

Thus, the savage man in a state of nature exists in peaceful ignorance of right and wrong, provides for his material needs and no more, is governed by his few and moderate passions, and generally has little reason to strive for anything more. Rousseau says at one point that man must have existed in this childlike state for many centuries before ever entering into society.

While Rousseau did not coin the phrase, these passages define the modern liberal concept of the "noble savage," and underlie liberal animosity towards industrialization.

Liberals often romanticize Native American peoples living in America before European colonization as equivalent to Rousseau's innocent, savage man. They like to represent them as noble conservationists, even when the evidence doesn't support that claim.

Many liberals also believe that Native American peoples avoided what Rousseau sees as the reason people leave the state of nature and enter civil society.

"THE first man who, having enclosed a piece of ground, bethought himself of saying This is mine, and found people simple enough to believe him, was the real founder of civil society. From how many crimes, wars and murders, from how many horrors and misfortunes might not any one have saved mankind, by pulling up the stakes, or filling up the ditch, and crying to his fellows, "Beware of listening to this impostor; you are undone if you once forget that the fruits of the earth belong to us all, and the earth itself to nobody."[7]

The point at which man begins to acquire property, both land and moveable property, is what Rousseau calls the "final stage in the state of nature." It is still the state of nature because man has not yet established government, but we are no longer dealing with "savage man." Man has by this time developed industry and engaged in the division of labor. For Hobbes these were blessings that could only be bestowed by government. For Rousseau they are a curse that leads to the inequality that necessitates government.

"So long as men remained content with their rustic huts, so long as they were satisfied with clothes made of the skins of animals and sewn together with thorns and fish-bones, adorned themselves only with feathers and shells, and continued to paint their bodies different colours, to improve and beautify their bows and arrows and to make with sharp-edged stones fishing boats or clumsy musical instruments; in a word, so long as they undertook only what a single person could accomplish, and confined themselves to such arts as did not require the joint labour of several hands, they lived free, healthy, honest and happy lives, so long as their nature allowed, and as they continued to enjoy the pleasures of mutual and independent intercourse. But from the moment one man began to stand in need of the help of another; from the moment it appeared advantageous to any one man to have enough provisions for two, equality disappeared, property was introduced, work became indispensable, and vast forests became smiling fields, which man had to water with the sweat of his brow, and where slavery and misery were soon seen to germinate and grow up with the crops."[8]

Once man begins to engage in the acquisition of property and the division of labor, he gives up the liberty and equality that he enjoyed in his savage state. Rousseau recognizes that every person will have different abilities and different ambitions, which will result in them acquiring unequal amounts of property. This destroys the tranquility of man's savage state and excites those more powerful passions that ultimately lead to a state of war.

"Finally, consuming ambition, the zeal for raising the relative level of his fortune, less out of real need than in order to put himself above others, inspires in all men a wicked tendency to harm one another, a secret jealousy all the more dangerous because, in order to strike its blow in greater safety, it often wears the mask of benevolence; in short, competition and rivalry on the one hand, opposition of interest[s] on the other, and always the hidden desire to profit at the expense of someone else. All these ills are the first effect of property and the inseparable offshoot of incipient inequality."[9]

Where man's dark nature and the natural state of war that exists between all men is the foundation of conservatism, *the inequality that results from any acquisition of property* is the foundation of liberalism. Socialists seek to abolish private property, democrats to heavily regulate and redistribute it, but both view the acquisition of property as inherently problematic.

This idea is also central to the romantic liberal view of the Native Americans before European colonization of the Americas. They often characterize them as living in that innocent, savage state, free of the corruption and conflict that ownership of property brings with it. We'll see later that this has no basis in reality.

For liberals, equality really is it. Nearly every political issue they take up has the word "equality" either explicitly or implicitly contained within it. They talk about "equal pay for equal work" for women. They fight for "marriage equality" for homosexuals. They complain about income equality in general, which is their explanation for all other societal ills, including "white privilege." Some people acquire more property than others and then use that advantage to oppress the rest.

It doesn't really matter to liberals *how* one has accumulated wealth. Rousseau does recognize that men may acquire property by different methods. He identifies the acquisition of property by force as a usurpation of the natural rights of man, which is not surprising. However, he sees the acquisition of property through honest labor in much the same way.

"Even those enriched exclusively by their industry could hardly base their property on better claims. They could very well say: 'I am the one who built that wall; I have earned this land with my labor.' In response to them it could be said: 'Who gave you the boundary lines? By what right do you claim to exact payment at our expense for labor we did not impose upon you? Are you unaware that a multitude of your brothers perish or suffer from need of what you have in excess, and that you needed explicit and unanimous consent from the human race for you to help yourself to anything from the common subsistence that went beyond your own?"[10]

Conservatives lost their minds when President Obama told business owners, "You didn't build that." As you can see, what he said was nothing new. He was drawing on fundamental liberal principles Rousseau articulated almost three hundred years ago.

Rousseau recognizes no natural right to property beyond what any human being absolutely needs for the preservation of himself and his dependents. He also views the acquisition of property as "a zero-sum game," meaning that no one can acquire anything without depriving someone else.

He argues that the earth and all of its resources belong to mankind in common, necessitating that any use of the land or its resources beyond what is needed to survive *requires the consent of all of mankind.*

French socialist Pierre-Joseph Proudhon famously echoed this idea, saying, "Property is Theft."[11]

Rousseau's ideas about property and inequality inspired the French Revolution, Marx, the 20th century communist movement, and the modern American liberal movement.

After identifying the advent of private property as the root of inequality and ultimately competition and war among men, Rousseau goes on to describe how men have in the past been deceived into consenting to governments that have preserved the unequal distribution of wealth. Once under the power of government, men were now bound by the laws of that government, which were written with the deliberate intent of preserving the wealth of the rich at the expense of the poor.

In other words, the government protected the 1% at the expense of the 99%.

Obedience to these laws returned the relative peace that existed in the state of nature, but not its relative equality. Marx will elaborate on these very ideas in constructing his theory.

Like Hobbes, Rousseau views those societies in a state of nature with all other societies. The inherent conflicts that occur between individuals within society led to war on a much grander scale. The source of all conflict is the acquisition of private property and the inequality that results from it.

Rousseau on the role of government

Identifying inequality as the great defect of the state of nature, Rousseau saw *restoring man's original equality as the purpose of government*. This is the underlying motivation for all liberal public policy. Where for conservatives it is security, for liberals it is equality, most importantly economic equality. Rousseau writes,

"It is to the law alone that men owe justice and liberty. It is this healthy tool of the will of all which reestablishes as a civil right the natural equality among men."[12]

Conservatives today complain that liberals do not just want equal rights, but equality of results. They're right. That's a fundamental liberal principle that goes back to Plato, but is also articulated here by Rousseau. The government must take an active role in changing the outcomes that would otherwise occur in a laissez faire economy. Even if the unequal distribution of wealth is due to unequal productivity, the government should address it.

While central, the quest for equality of results is by no means limited to economic results. Liberals seek to ensure that every individual, regardless of differences in gender, race, creed or sexual orientation, have equality of results in all aspects of life. This is the motivation for positive laws regarding social and economic interactions between the majority and minority groups liberals see as disadvantaged or oppressed.

When a conservative baker declined to prepare a wedding cake for a gay marriage, liberals sought legal penalties. According to their worldview, the gay couple had a right to equal treatment with heterosexuals by the baker. Where even many non-liberals support the right of homosexual people to get married, true liberals go farther. They insist on positive laws that prohibit anyone from refusing to associate with homosexuals.

The government does not just recognize an inherent political equality in all human beings. It must take positive steps to ensure equal results for all members of society. There is no conflict any individual's inherent rights, because those were all surrendered to the general will upon formation of the society. That's completely antithetical to the American Creed, but it's the way liberals think and it affects the way they react to real world situations like this one.

Rousseau on the extent of government power

Having defined the purpose of government, Rousseau proceeds to the extent of its powers. Like Hobbes, Rousseau makes a clear distinction between the powers vested in government and the form that it takes. He similarly devotes a chapter of his treatise *On the Social Contract* to explaining the sovereign power.

Although the purpose of government is entirely different for Rousseau, his ideas about the sovereign power are remarkably similar to Hobbes.' Most significantly, Rousseau believes that man has to *give up all of his natural rights* to the sovereign power when entering the social contract, in return for the benefits that contract will bestow. He summarizes the "clauses" of the social contract to one.

"These clauses, properly understood, are all reducible to a single one, namely the *total alienation* of each associate, together with all of his rights, to the entire community."[13]

Rousseau is kind to our investigation in using precisely the same word as the American Creed. Rights cannot be both "unalienable" and "alienable" at the same time. On this point alone, liberals depart from the Creed completely.

In exchange for giving up his natural rights, man in society will be granted "civil rights," which are really government-granted privileges. According to Rousseau, this is necessary because if man retained his natural rights while a party to the social contract, he would eventually claim to be his own judge, thus undermining the social contract and returning man to the state of nature.

Rousseau concludes that there is an immediate equality in this renunciation, as each individual has given up the same rights and assumed the same power over everyone else. He goes so far as to demonstrate this with mathematical calculations, asserting that in a city of 10,000 citizens, each individual citizen has $1/10,000^{th}$ of the power. Each individual pledges his portion of this power to the good of the state, which is now dedicated to what Rousseau calls "the general will."

"Each of us places his person and all his power in common under the supreme direction of the general will; and as one we receive each member as an indivisible part of the whole."[14]

In order for the government to successfully execute this "general will," Rousseau also argues, like Hobbes, that the sovereign power must be absolute, indivisible, and inalienable.

"Just as nature gives each man an absolute power over all his members, the social compact gives the body politic an absolute power over all its members, and it is the same power which, as I have said, is directed by the general will and bears the name sovereignty."[15]

"I therefore maintain that since sovereignty is merely the exercise of the general will, it can never be alienated, and that the sovereign, which is only a collective being, cannot be represented by anything but itself. Power can perfectly well be transmitted, but not the will."[16]

"Sovereignty is indivisible for the same reason that it is inalienable. For either the will is general, or it is not. It is the will of either the people as a whole or of only a part."[17]

While there are some superficial differences between Hobbes and Rousseau concerning the powers vested in the sovereign, for both that power is absolute. While Rousseau will go on to suggest a different form of government than does Hobbes, the powers exercised are the same.

One specific power Rousseau identifies explicitly in *Political Economy* is that of controlling the amount of wealth that any of its citizens can accumulate.

"It is one of the most important items of business for the government to prevent extreme inequality of fortunes, not by appropriating treasures from their owners, but by denying everyone the means of acquiring them, and not by building hospitals for the poor but by protecting citizens from becoming poor."[18]

Here Rousseau lays the foundation for a modern liberal society. Private property is not abolished, but heavy regulation prevents extreme concentrations of wealth on the one hand and extreme poverty on the other. Thus so does government achieve its prime directive: to remedy the inequality caused by man's acquisition of private property. Rousseau does not rule out redistribution (there are no limits on the legislative power of the majority), but prefers preventative measures as more effective than attempting to solve economic inequality once it already exists.

Under this system, the individual has no natural right to keep the fruits of his labor without the consent of all mankind, as Rousseau established earlier. Ultimately, the state will indirectly decide how the product of each person's labor is distributed through the democratic process.

Rousseau on education

Rousseau also identifies public education as one of the core functions of legitimate government. Rousseau argues that you cannot have liberty without virtue, and that you cannot have virtue unless you teach your citizens to be virtuous, which he defines as absolute loyalty to the state. Rousseau goes so far as to say that by educating children on their duties as citizens, the state teaches them how "to deserve to live."

"If, for example, they are trained early enough never to consider their own persons except in terms of being related to the body of the state, and not to perceive their own existence except as part of the state's existence, they will eventually come to identify themselves in some way with this larger whole, to feel themselves to be members of the country, to love it with that exquisite sentiment that every isolated man feels only for himself, to elevate their soul perpetually toward this great object, and thus to transform into a sublime virtue this dangerous disposition from which arises all our vices."[19]

Importantly, Rousseau argues that this duty to educate the children "to obey others" cannot be executed solely by the family, under the leadership of the father. Rousseau argues that the state has a larger stake in the education of the child, since the father will eventually die while the state will live on. Therefore, the state should replace the father as the party responsible for the education of the child and determine what that education should consist of. Since they are only exercising the "general will," of which the father is a part, Rousseau concludes that the father should have no reason to object!

This is why Hillary Clinton says "it takes a village to raise a child." It actually goes back to Plato, who wanted his "guardians" educated by the state. It's a lot creepier when you really understand what she means!

A role for the state in educating children is another plank that both conservatives and liberals have in common. Conservatives seek to have the state promote religious values, while liberals seek to have the state promote secular ones.

In both cases, education is more than just "reading, writing and arithmetic." The principle objective of education for both Hobbes and Rousseau is to indoctrinate children with the beliefs and values that will best serve the state. To do so, the state's values must combine with or replace the parents'.

It also explains the latest controversy over "Common Core." If you listen carefully, neither conservatives nor liberals seem to object to the fundamental principle: the centralized control over the content of child education in mandatory education. They just disagree over what that content is and how to teach it.

How many social media posts or articles have you seen criticizing the overly complicated way Common Core attempts to teach math? Too many to mention.

Now, how many have you seen criticizing Common Core for having children read government manuals, with all their attendant propaganda? Or criticizing Common Core on its basic premise, that the central government should dictate the methods and content of child education? Outside of a few honest constitutional conservatives, almost none at all.

To his credit, conservative commentator Bill Whittle calls Common Core what it is: Orwell's "Ministry of Truth."

With regard to religion, which is directly related to education in that it affects how the person thinks about his relationship to the state, Rousseau at first seems slightly less authoritarian. He argues that the rights of the sovereign do not go beyond what is necessary to the common good of the state. Therefore, the particular religion that any citizen practices is of no concern to the sovereign, *as long as* that religion "causes him to love his duties."

To the extent practice of his particular religion exhorts the citizen to go over and above his duties to the state, without neglecting those duties or otherwise harming the state, each citizen is free to do as he pleases in this area. However, Rousseau actually talks about another kind of religion that is mandatory for every citizen.

"There is, therefore, a purely civil profession of faith, the articles of which it belongs to the sovereign to establish, not exactly as dogmas of religion, but as sentiments of sociability, without which it is impossible to be a good citizen or a faithful subject. While not having the ability to obligate anyone to believe them, the sovereign can banish from the state anyone who does not believe them. It can banish him not for being impious but for being unsociable, for being incapable of sincerely loving the laws and justice, and of sacrificing his life, if necessary, for his duty. If, after having publicly acknowledged these same dogmas, a person acts as if he does not believe them, he should be put to death; he has committed the greatest of crimes: he has lied before the laws."[20]

You'll often hear conservatives say that liberals replace God with government. It sounds like they're right about that, too.

Rousseau on the form of government

For Rousseau, the sovereign also has the legislative power, which should at all times reflect the general will. Unlike Hobbes, however, Rousseau does not believe that the executive power should be wielded by the sovereign. The executive power is the agent that carries into effect the general will and is subordinate to it.

"What then is the government? An intermediate body established between the subjects and the sovereign for their mutual communication, and charged with the execution of the laws and the preservation of liberty, both civil and political."[21]

Rousseau goes on to explain that the government consists of magistrates or kings and gives them the general name "prince," which he uses to refer to the government, in whatever form it takes. So, when Rousseau says "government" he really means "executive branch."

For Rousseau, even a prince is merely an agent of the sovereign, which is the people, and cannot exercise any arbitrary authority over them. The prince's role is to execute the general will. If the executive substitutes its own will for the general will, it has exercised illegitimate power.

Rousseau asserts that an equilibrium must be achieved, then, between the power of the government over the people and the power of the people. The people are both sovereign as a whole and subjects individually. Individually, they have given up all of their rights, power, and even their will to the state.

It goes without saying that this is completely antithetical to the American Creed. But it's implicit in nearly all liberal rhetoric. How many times have you heard liberals answer a criticism about government overreach with the rejoinder, "That's why we have elections?" For liberals, there is no government overreach as long as a majority vote sanctioned the policy.

As to the form that the government should take, Rousseau says that all states which are ultimately subject to "the rule of law" are republics. However, Rousseau does not argue for a representative republic, as he maintains that the sovereign power cannot be represented. Instead, the whole people exercise the legislative power through legislators, who possess neither the legislative power nor the executive power themselves. They are merely professional lawmakers, employed as agents of the people. The legislators draft the laws, which are passed by the whole people and executed by the government.

Since there must be some way to discover the general will in order to exercise it through legislation, Rousseau asserts that this is accomplished through majority vote. While the social contract itself must be unanimous, with anyone who does not consent to it excluded from the contract (and forced to leave the territory), all acts of sovereignty under the social contract are determined by the will of the majority.

For Rousseau, this is not a means for each individual to give his consent, which he has already given to the sovereign power over everything, but rather to discover what the general will is.

This interpretation of the nature of voting and legislating allows Rousseau to give a bizarre though convenient answer to the question of whether the minority has any recourse to legislation that they disagree with.

"When, therefore, the opinion contrary to mine prevails, this proves merely that I was in error, and that what I took to be the general will was not so. If my private opinion had prevailed, I would have done something other than what I had wanted. In that case I would have not been free."[22]

Seriously, he just said that any opinion the majority doesn't endorse must be an error. It's a good thing Copernicus and Galileo didn't think this way!

More importantly, Rousseau's thinking here is completely antithetical to the Bill of Rights. Those amendments were written with the express purpose of protecting the individual against the majority. In fact, the whole constitutional system of separated and strictly enumerated powers was designed to protect individuals against the kind of absolute democracy Rousseau advocates.

At first glance, Rousseau's philosophy might look to some to be more closely related to the ideals of the American republic than Hobbes.' Rather than an absolute monarch, Rousseau advocates for a democratic republic, with the power reserved to the people, who exercise it by electing a government to carry out their will. The goal of the republic is liberty and equality for all, which is accomplished by subjecting both the citizens and the government to the rule of law.

There is only one problem. While his government is organized in a completely different manner than Hobbes,' it is quite the same by the most important measurement: the power that it yields. Like Hobbes, Rousseau concludes that in order to accomplish its daunting task, the state must have absolute power over its citizens. While each of them has a small, proportionate share in that power, no one of them has any right to resist.

The "general will," represented by the will of the majority, supplants the will of every individual in society. The majority decides how children are to be educated and thus what they think. The majority makes rules about how much property any individual can accumulate. Each individual *gives up all of his natural rights* and allows the majority to determine what "civil liberties" he is allowed.

These ideas are completely irreconcilable with the American creed, where rights are inalienable, where each individual has a right to pursue *his own* happiness, and where his thoughts, speech, and religious beliefs are beyond the reach of government.

It probably goes without saying that we won't find them in Marx, either. But it's important to understand where Marx departs from Rousseau to understand the difference between democrats and socialists within the liberal movement.

While Rousseau provides the philosophical foundation for modern liberalism, the influence of Marx cannot be denied. There are too many similarities between modern liberal rhetoric and policy and Marx's ideas, particularly as expressed in the *Communist Manifesto* and *Das Kapital*. Yet, many 20th century American liberals were fierce opponents of communism. How can both be true?

The answer is somewhat analogous to the differences between Hobbes and Burke. While expressing them in more socio-economic terms, Marx substantively agrees with most of Rousseau's philosophical assumptions, especially his view of private property. Marx departs from Rousseau merely in his ideas about what political action is necessary to resolve the problems caused by private property.

Marx on the nature of man

In the *Manifesto*, Marx famously wrote, "The history of all hitherto existing societies is the history of class struggles."[23] The idea of history being a series of epochs in which different property structures resulted in different class struggles is central to Marx's argument. But Engels' 1888 footnote to this iconic statement provides even more insight.

"That is, all written history. In 1847, the prehistory of society, the social organization existing previous to recorded history, was all but unknown. Since then, Haxthausen discovered common ownership of land in Russia, Maurer proved it to be the social foundation from which all Teutonic races started in history, and by and by the village communities were found to be, or to have been, the primitive form of society everywhere from India to Ireland. The inner organization of this primitive Communistic society was laid bare, in its typical form, by Morgan's crowning discovery of the true nature of the gens and its relation to the tribe. With the dissolution of these primeval communities society begins to be differentiated into separate and finally antagonistic classes. I have attempted to retrace this process of dissolution in 'The Origin of the Family, Private Property and the State." (Chicago, Charles H. Kerr & Co.)[24]

This is substantively the same as Rousseau's view of prehistoric man. Between his "savage man" period and the creation of government, Rousseau also claimed there was a period where men lived in "rustic huts" and claimed for themselves only "what a single person could accomplish, and confined themselves to such arts as did not require the joint labour of several hands." While in this state, human beings "lived free, healthy, honest and happy lives."

Marx, like Rousseau, sees private property and the division of labor as the root causes of conflict. Marx merely develops the idea with more emphasis on the different class struggles he believes define historical epochs.

"In ancient Rome we have patricians, knights, plebeians, slaves; in the Middle Ages, feudal lords, vassals, guild masters, journeymen, apprentices, serfs; in almost all of these classes, again, subordinate gradations.

The modern bourgeois society that has sprouted from the ruins of feudal society has not done away with class antagonisms. It has but established new classes, new conditions of oppression, new forms of struggle in place of the old ones."[25]

This is really no different than Rousseau's ideas about how men had been deceived in the past by governments that perpetuated the inequalities among men. Marx just comes up with new marketing for it, labeling them "class struggles."

Marx on the purpose of government

The root of the problem for Marx is the same as for Rousseau: the inequality that results from any acquisition of private property. Marx differs only in how to solve it. Marx regards the prescriptions of Rousseau and his more direct philosophical descendants like Proudhon as inadequate and unrealistic, dismissing them as "appeal to the feelings and purses of the bourgeois."[26]

Marx believes only full scale revolution will suffice. The present property structure epoch of bourgeois and proletariat must be completely overthrown and replaced by the new and final epoch, where the proletariat rules directly and finally eliminates class struggle as the fundamental dynamic of human society.

"The distinguishing feature of Communism is not the abolition of property generally, but the abolition of bourgeois property. But modern bourgeois private property is the final most complete expression of the system of producing and appropriating products that is based on class antagonisms, on the exploitation of the many by the few.

In this sense, the theory of the Communists may be summed up in the single sentence: Abolition of private property."[27]

It might be argued that the complete abolition of private property is a departure from Rousseau, not only in means but in ends. However, both Rousseau and Marx are after the same thing: economic equality. The difference is merely one of degree. Rousseau believes a tolerable amount of economic equality can be achieved through heavy regulation of private property through legislation. Marx believes equality is only achieved with the elimination of private property completely.

Moreover, as Rousseau did not construct a complex economic theory that compares with Marx's, one could argue that Rousseau's all-powerful democracy could certainly execute Marx's plan.

Marx on the form of government

Still, Marx certainly anticipates the need for more radical change and more authoritarianism than Rousseau admits to anywhere in his writing. Where Rousseau says "A country cannot exist without liberty," Marx is more realistic about what is necessary to achieve equality of outcomes:

"The proletariat will use its political supremacy to wrest, by degrees, all capital from the bourgeoisie, to centralise all instruments of production in the hands of the State, i.e., of the proletariat organised as the ruling class; and to increase the total of productive forces as rapidly as possible.

Of course, in the beginning, *this cannot be effected except by means of despotic inroads on the rights of property*, and on the conditions of bourgeois production; by means of measures, therefore, which appear economically insufficient and untenable, but which, in the course of the movement, outstrip themselves, necessitate further inroads upon the old social order, and are unavoidable as a means of entirely revolutionizing the mode of production."[28] [emphasis added]

While Marx openly admits the need for a despotic government, run by the proletariat, in order to abolish private property and institute a new mode of production, he believes this despotism will be temporary. As government itself is merely "the organised power of one class for oppressing another,"[29] Marx believes that once the proletariat has created a classless society, it will have eliminated the need for government. The result will be an anarchistic society "in which the free development of each is the condition for the free development of all."[30]

Conclusion

As with the American conservative movement, there are generally two groups of liberals. Both accept Rousseau's views on the nature of man and the inherent problems resulting from the acquisition of private property, primarily inequality of condition.

Like conservatives, they also believe all men are created equal, but understand that equality to mean something completely different than does the American Creed.

They do not believe rights are inalienable. They believe rights must be totally alienated as a condition of entering society.

As they do not believe in inalienable rights, they do not agree with the American Creed on the purpose of government. Instead of securing rights, the purpose of government is to restore man's natural equality, which is lost the moment he begins acquiring private property.

Liberal democrats believe in unlimited democracy, or a government with absolute power, as long as that power is sanctioned by majority vote. This is something the founding fathers consistently denounced. As James Madison wrote,

"Hence it is that such democracies have ever been spectacles of turbulence and contention; have ever been found incompatible with personal security or the rights of property; and have in general been as short in their lives as they have been violent in their deaths."[31]

Socialists believe unlimited democracy is inadequate to solve the problems of inequality, restated as "class warfare," caused by the acquisition of private property. Only state control of the means of production and abolition of the market economy can restore true equality.

The distinction between the two groups is by no means absolute. It is hard to find liberals who do not support the idea of "single payer" health care, meaning government ownership of the means of production of healthcare services. At the very least, they see an inherent conflict in health care being delivered on a for profit basis.

In conclusion, you cannot reconcile the liberal philosophy with the American Creed. Like conservatism, it is completely antithetical.

This leaves us with an interesting problem. We seem to have run out of philosophies in American politics. If both conservatism and liberalism flatly contradict the American Creed, we are left with a very important question:

What philosophy inspired the American Revolution and where did its adherents go?

Chapter Four:

Where Did the Founding Fathers Come From?

"Resolved, that it is the opinion of this Board that as to the general principles of liberty and the rights of man, in nature and in society, the doctrines of Locke, in his "Essay concerning the true original extent and end of civil government," and of Sidney in his "Discourses on government," may be considered as those generally approved by our fellow citizens of this, and the United States,"

– Thomas Jefferson (1825)[1]

The term "founding father" is often used rather loosely. In popular culture, even Lincoln is sometimes given this title, despite living almost a century after the founding. There is a more serious distinction between the fifty-six men who signed the Declaration of Independence in 1776 and the thirty-nine who signed the U.S. Constitution thirteen years later, although there is some overlap between the two.

As far as the Constitution is concerned, Kevin Gutzman, Ph.D. astutely observes that the so-called "framers" of the Constitution "had no legal effect at all. The ratifiers, on the other hand, were the people who put the Constitution into effect; it was their act that made it binding, and their understanding that is significant."[2]

So who were the founding fathers? For our purposes, we'll define the founding of the United States as having occurred in 1776, with the resolution by Congress on July 2 to legally dissolve all political ties with Great Britain. While the colonists would have to defend this resolution on the battlefield for the next seven years, it was never overturned. The parties to that resolution, along with the millions who generally shared their views, were the true "founding fathers."

Two days after the resolution, Congress approved the Declaration of Independence, considered the definitive statement of America's founding principles. While Thomas Jefferson is recognized as the "author" of that document, it by no means represented solely his views. He prepared the first draft, but the content of the Declaration was heavily edited by Congress. One must conclude that the document in its final form generally represented the views of most of the members of that body.

There were exceptions. John Dickinson opposed separation at that time altogether and refused to sign. We'll see that John Adams didn't necessarily agree completely with all of the philosophical tenets of the famous preamble. But most of them did agree, or they would have included changes to it among their numerous revisions.

In contrast, Jefferson *was* merely expressing his own opinion in the prologue to this chapter, although he was successful in getting the University of Virginia to adopt his resolution. He cited John Locke as the source of America's founding principles on more than one occasion and often referred to him as one of the "three greatest men the world has ever produced." As far as he was concerned, Locke was the foundation for American liberty. But was he right?

Understanding the Locke essay Jefferson cited would seem helpful in answering the question posed by the title of this chapter.[3] We've seen that both conservatism and liberalism reject the principles expressed in the Declaration of Independence. If we can reasonably establish that Locke is their source, it would be fair to conclude that Jefferson was generally correct.

Locke and the Declaration of Independence

Writing almost forty years after Hobbes' first publication of *Leviathan* and sixty years before Rousseau, John Locke wrote his *Two Treatises of Civil Government* to accomplish two goals. The first treatise was written to refute the arguments of Sir Robert Filmer, who argued for absolute monarchy in his *Patriarcha*, published posthumously in 1680.

Unlike Hobbes, who made his argument empirically, Filmer built his argument for absolute monarchy around the revealed word of the scriptures. He concluded that the legitimate sovereignty of the monarchs of the various countries could be traced back to the sovereignty God granted Adam at the dawn of creation.

Filmer's argument rests upon the assumption that all government power derives from paternal power, the father's legitimate authority to rule over his children. This authority is passed on to his heirs, and Filmer traces the rule of the various monarchs back through history as presented in the Bible to Adam, who was granted authority over all of the earth by God.

Locke's First Treatise of Government, entitled, "The False Principles and Foundation of Sir Robert Filmer, And His Followers, are Detected and Overthrown," refutes Filmer on his own terms. As the divine right of kings is no longer a position that has any standing, we will concentrate on Locke's Second Treatise, "Essay Concerning the True Original Extent and End of Civil Government." In this second essay, Locke constructs his own view of the state of nature and builds his arguments for government from there.

Locke on the nature of man and the natural law

Like Hobbes, Locke's first observation about the state of nature is man's natural liberty and equality.

"To understand political power right, and derive it from its original, we must consider, what state all men are naturally in, and that is, a state of perfect freedom to order their actions and dispose of their possessions and persons, as they think fit, within the bounds of the law of nature, without asking leave, or depending upon the will of any other man.

A state also of equality, wherein all the power and jurisdiction is reciprocal, no one having more than another; there being nothing more evident, than that creatures of the same species and rank, promiscuously born to all the same advantages of nature, and the use of the same faculties, should also be equal one amongst another without subordination or subjection, unless the lord and master of them all, by any manifest declaration of his will, set one above another, and confer on him, by and evident and clear appointment, an undoubted right to dominion and sovereignty."[4]

Notice the immediate contrast with both Hobbes and Rousseau. Hobbes asserted that man's liberty in the state of nature had no bounds, resulting in a state of war. Rousseau argued it was bound only by man's natural pity for his fellow man. Locke's position refutes both. Man's liberty in the state of nature has a natural limit, which is what he calls "the law of nature."

What is the law of nature?

"The state of nature has a law of nature to govern it, which obliges everyone: and reason, which is that law, teaches all mankind, who will but consult it, that being all equal and independent, no one ought to harm another in his life, health, liberty, or possessions."[5]

Locke on the natural rights

The natural limit on man's actions in the state of nature is that no person should harm another in his life, health, liberty, or possessions. This is what many political theorists today call the *non-aggression principle*; that each person is free to do whatever he wishes as long as he does not infringe upon the rights of others. The reverse side of this principle is that no man has a right to use force against another human being unless he is defending himself against previous aggression.

Locke also observes that all men are born equal for roughly the same reasons as both Hobbes and Rousseau. They all have "the same advantages of nature," meaning physical strength and ability is more or less equal, and all have "use of the same faculties," meaning the differences in innate intelligence are negligible. Therefore, there is no natural justification for one man to wield power over another. However, like his take on natural liberty, Locke's view of the consequences of man's basic equality is diametrically opposed to Hobbes.'

"This equality of men by nature, the judicious Hooker looks upon as so evident in itself, and beyond all question, that he makes it the foundation of that obligation to mutual love amongst men, on which he builds the duties they owe one another, and from whence he derives the great maxims of justice and charity."[6]

One could not imagine a more striking contrast. For Hobbes, the consequence of man's basic equality is war; for Locke, love. Indeed, Locke's view of the state of nature on the whole is completely opposite of Hobbes'. Where Hobbes equates the state of nature with the state of war, Locke explicitly distinguishes the state of nature from the state of war.

"And here we have the plain difference between the state of nature and the state of war, *which however some men have confounded*, are as far distant, as a state of peace, good will, mutual assistance and preservation, and a state of enmity, malice, violence and mutual destruction are from one another. Men living together according to reason, without a common superior on earth, with authority to judge between them, is properly the state of nature. But force, or a declared design of force, upon the person of another, where there is no common superior on earth to appeal to for relief, is the state of war: and it is the want of such an appeal gives a man the right of war even against an aggressor, *though he be in society and a fellow subject*."[emphasis added]

This is no mere difference in semantics. Locke completely departs from Hobbes view of the nature of man. Locke does not see man as a depraved creature whose natural inclination is to wage war against his fellow man.

Locke separates the state of nature from the state of war to illustrate that the state of war, which is defined by the initiation of force, or aggression, is *unnatural* to man.

Neither does Locke consider man's natural state to be the "blissful ignorance" described by Rousseau, wherein savage man is barely aware of his own children or of any sense of morality. For Locke, man's natural state is reason, by which he implicitly understands the non-aggression principle as following from the eternal law of nature.

Locke also recognizes the natural right for every human being to defend himself against the aggression of another, which was Hobbes' second law of nature. He includes the clarification "though he be in society and a fellow subject." This is the first indication of another key difference between Locke and the other two philosophers made explicit by Locke in later chapters.

While Hobbes and Rousseau both asserted man had to give up all of his natural rights to the sovereign power when entering society, Locke maintains that man carries most of his natural rights with him into society, and that protection of those natural rights is the sole purpose of government.

Finally, we have a philosophy that recognizes the existence of natural, inalienable rights. The idea that some rights are inalienable, that they cannot be taken away by another, nor even given away by man himself, is central to Locke's treatise. It is also one of the "self-evident" truths in the American Declaration of Independence.

Locke truly departs from both Hobbes and Rousseau on the subject of property. Hobbes said it does not even exist in the state of nature. Rousseau says it exists but is the source of all human conflict.

Locke argues that property ownership does indeed exist in nature and is not only a good thing, but essential to human survival.

So how do you acquire the right own any particular thing? Locke says it derives from self-ownership:

"Though the earth, and all inferior creatures, be common to all men, *yet every man has a property in his own person*: this no body has any right to but himself. The labour of his body, and the work of his hands, we may say, are properly his. Whatsoever then he removes out of the state that nature hath provided, and left it in, he hath mixed his labour with, and joined to it something that is his own, and thereby makes it his property."[7]

There are more "haths" and "whatsoevers" in this passage, but it's vitally important. Let's translate it.

Every individual owns himself. This is a basic assumption that Locke considers self-evident and it's hard to argue against it. Given our definition of ownership, who else could possibly have a right to decide what you do with your own body?

If you own yourself, then you must own your labor, the results of you exercising property rights in your own body. Not only does this require effort; it requires time. Your time. Time that you have a limited supply of while on this earth, just as you have a limited supply of money. It's no accident that we use the word "spent" to describe the depletion of both.

So, when you spend your time and effort to remove something out of the state of nature, provided it does not already belong to someone else, you have a right to own that thing. You have "bought" it with the labor you spent.

Locke then directly refutes Rousseau's assertion that doing so is a theft:

"And will any one say, he had no right to those acorns or apples, he thus appropriated, because he had not the consent of all mankind to make them his? Was it a robbery thus to assume to himself what belonged to all in common? If such a consent as that was necessary, man had starved, notwithstanding the plenty God had given him. We see in commons, which remain so by compact, that it is the taking any part of what is common, and removing it out of the state nature leave it in, which begins the property; without which the common is of no use. And the taking of this or that part, does not depend on the express consent of all the commoners....The labour that was mine, removing them out of that common state they were in, hath fixed my property in them."[8]

"No body could think himself injured by the drinking of another man, though he took a good draught, who had a whole river of the same water left him to quench his thirst: and the case of land and water, where there is enough of both, is perfectly the same."[9]

Think of three people stranded on a desert island. There is a finite amount of fruit on the island's trees, but there is more than the three people could ever eat. So, no matter what any one of them takes, there is enough left for the other two. Does any one of them need the permission of the other two to wander into the forest and pick fruit to eat? Locke says no. If they did, they wouldn't really have a right to life, would they? Each person's life would now be a privilege granted by the other two, because either of the other two could stop them from eating by refusing permission to pick any fruit.

When you start thinking about a much larger area or the whole world, you can see Locke's point about man starving if he needed permission from every individual before he took ownership of any food. The same reasoning applies to materials for clothing or shelter. Ownership of property, even in the state of nature, is essential to man's survival. That and the fact that acquiring and disposing of the fruits of your own labor does not constitute harm to others makes it a natural *right*.

This is another complete break from conservatives and liberals, who each regard property ownership as a privilege granted by the government, although they each get there by different routes.

Locke also departs from Hobbes and Rousseau on contracts in the state of nature. Hobbes believed they would never be honored, while Rousseau's "noble savage" is barely aware of his fellow creatures, much less entering into contracts with them. Locke's view refutes them both:

"The promises and bargains between the two men in the desert island, mentioned by Garcilasso de la Vega, in his history of Peru: or between a Swiss and an Indian, in the woods of America, are binding to them, though they are perfectly in a state of nature, in reference to one another: for truth and keeping of faith belongs to men, as men, and not as members of society."[10]

In summary, Locke's view of man in nature departs from both conservatives and liberals on every substantive point.

While Hobbes recognizes man's basic equality, he believes equality is the source of war. Locke says it is the source of love. Hobbes asserts that in nature man has a right to everything, even including other people's bodies.

Rousseau argues that man's liberty is limited only by his pity for the suffering of others. Locke states that man's natural liberty is limited by reason, which prohibits aggression.

Hobbes says property is impossible in the state of nature; Locke says it is not only possible, but without it, the human species *would never have survived*.

This is not to say Locke does not recognize the dangers inherent in the state of nature. He recognizes men will not always adhere to the natural law of non-aggression, and for this reason they agree to enter society and put themselves under government.

Where Hobbes saw man in nature as completely depraved, Locke sees him as capable of both peaceful cooperation and war and plunder. He is inclined to the former, but capable of the latter under the right circumstances.

He also disagrees with Rousseau's argument that man's acquisition of property in the state of nature is harmful to others.

Locke on the role of government

Locke concludes that, although not a de facto state of war, the state of nature makes "the enjoyment of the property he has in this state very unsafe, very insecure."[11]

"This makes him willing to quit a condition, which, however free, is full of fears and continual dangers: and it is not without reason, that he seeks out, and is willing to join in society with others, who are already united, or have a mind to unite, for the mutual preservation of their lives, liberties and estates, which I call by the name, property.

The great and chief end, therefore, of men's uniting into commonwealths, and putting themselves under government, is the preservation of their property."[12]

The contrast here with Rousseau could not be more striking. The purpose of government is not to correct the inequality caused by the acquisition of property, it is to preserve property itself!

Again, we see Locke using the word "preserve." It's important because he is the only one of the philosophers we've looked at who believes there is anything good about nature.

For both Hobbes and Rousseau, the purpose of government is to completely eradicate the conditions of the state of nature and, more importantly, to override man's natural inclinations for the good of society. They see man's natural inclinations as depraved or destructive. That is why the government's power must be absolute; because it must completely overcome every individual's will.

In contrast, Locke by no means wants government to eradicate all elements of the state of nature nor to dominate man's natural inclinations. He sees man as naturally inclined to reason and views his natural equality, liberty, and justly acquired property as not only beneficial but essential to survival. The purpose of government, then, is to *preserve* those aspects of the state of nature that allow men to thrive and pursue their happiness and to allow them to follow their natural inclinations in peace and safety.

The word "preserve" is also consistent with Locke's position that man does not give up his natural rights upon entering society, but instead carries them with him.

Locke on the extent of government power

Given this vastly different purpose for government, the next question concerns what powers Locke believes should be invested in government in order to allow it to fulfill its mission. For both Hobbes and Rousseau, the sovereign power must be absolute, indivisible, and inalienable.

Again, Locke is a polar opposite He never even mentions the word "sovereignty" in relation to government in his entire treatise. In his system, government power must be limited, divided, and subject to revocation by the people whenever it is misused.

Let us first examine the Locke's statement of the powers vested in government. He consolidates the powers man has in the state of nature into two. It is from these two basic powers that he derives the powers of government.

"The first power, viz. of doing whatsoever be thought for the preservation of himself, and the rest of mankind, he gives up to be regulated by laws made by the society, so far forth as the preservation of himself, and the rest of that society shall require; which laws of the society in many things confine the liberty he had by the law of nature.

Secondly, the power of punishing he wholly gives up, and engages his natural force, (which he might before employ in the execution of the law of nature, by his own single authority, as he thought fit) to assist the executive power of the society, as the law thereof shall require..."[13]

The vesting of these two basic powers in government, to make laws and punish crimes, resolves what Locke views as the three defects of the law of nature: first, that without defined laws, men's biases or ignorance will lead them to misinterpret the law of nature; second, that there is no indifferent judge in the state of nature, leaving every man a judge in his own case; and third, that not everyone can defend themselves on their own, leaving the guilty unpunished for violating the law of nature.

Already there is an important distinction between the two powers. Notice that the power to make laws that "confine" man's natural liberty is limited to making laws "so far forth as the preservation of himself, and the rest of that society shall require."

So, the government cannot make any laws it pleases, but only those which *preserve*. This is in contrast to the power to punish crimes, which Locke says men *wholly* give up to the government. Locke says man in nature has a natural right to punish crimes, which is the power to use force upon others *after they have committed a crime against him*; in other words, after they have committed aggression.

That is the source of both the executive and legislative power. Until aggression has been committed, man has no right to use force against another.

It is also important to separate the concepts of "powers" and "rights." Man gives up powers when entering society, but never gives up rights.

This is important in understanding Locke's limitations on the power of the state. While Locke says the legislative power is the supreme power in society, which everyone in society is obliged to obey, he clearly defines the limits of that power:

"A man, as has been proved, cannot subject himself to the arbitrary power of another; and having in the state of nature no arbitrary power over the life, liberty, or possession of another, but only so much as the law of nature gave him for the preservation of himself, and the rest of mankind; *this is all he doth, or can give up to the commonwealth*, and by it to the legislative power, so that the legislative can have no more than this."[14] [emphasis added]

This is quite an astounding statement about the limit of government power; that it is limited to the power any one person has over another in the state of nature. Locke has already defined government as the societal use of force, where every man "engages his natural force" to assist the executive in enforcing the laws. Man is prohibited in nature from ever initiating force and from harming another in his life, health, liberty, or possessions. He may only use force in self-defense against aggression, when an aggressor has initiated a state of war.

Therefore, government power has the same limits. Laws, which are backed by force, can only be made to prohibit aggression by one person or group against another, thereby *preserving* life, liberty, and property. As Locke goes on to say, "The obligations of the law of nature *cease not in society*, but only in many cases are drawn closer, and have by human laws known penalties annexed to them, to enforce their observation."[15] [emphasis added]

So, the "law of nature" is preserved as well.

Where both Hobbes and Rousseau gave the sovereign unlimited power, the power of government for Locke could not be more limited. It literally has no power over the individual in society unless he commits an act of aggression against another. It can only defend the individual's rights to life, liberty, and property and can never violate them.

It is this idea that is succinctly stated in the Declaration's preamble: "That to secure these rights, governments are instituted among men." Governments are not instituted to repress man's depraved inclinations or to artificially achieve economic equality. For the signers of that document, the purpose of government was the same as it was for Locke.

A further conclusion that can be drawn from this argument is that the legislative power is in all cases limited to a negative power. In other words, it can only prohibit certain behavior, but cannot *require* any behavior. Hobbes and Rousseau both vested their governments with the power to force men to be virtuous. For Locke, this power is reserved for God. The laws of men may only prohibit aggression.

Locke on education

These limitations on government power also apply to education. Hobbes and Rousseau both invested the sovereign with the power to dictate how children would be educated, with the ultimate goal being to teach them to be loyal to the sovereign. Interestingly, the only chapter in Locke's Second Treatise that even contains the word "sovereign" is his chapter on "Paternal Power."[16] In this chapter he uses the word "sovereignty" only to briefly refute Filmer again. He goes on to make his arguments about what powers parents have over their children.

For Locke, the parents exercise only a temporary "sovereignty" over their children, during the period when the children's reason has not developed sufficiently for them to exercise their natural liberty. For Locke, the natural limit of liberty is reason. Before their reason is fully developed, children must obey their parents. However, when they have come to an age and stage of their education where they are capable of understanding and applying the law of nature, they become equals with their parents and claim a full right to their natural liberty.

Unlike Hobbes and Rousseau, Locke acknowledges no legitimate authority of the state to interfere with the education of children. This right is reserved solely to the parents. The parents may agree to allow other people to educate their children (Locke cites apprenticeship as an example), but the ultimate decision about who, what, where, and when their children are educated remains solely with the parents. Children are literally beyond the reach of the state, only becoming part of society when they are mature enough in their reason to choose to join society.

With these limits on its power, redistribution of wealth is off limits to the government. Since man cannot initiate force against another in nature in order to "harm him in his possessions," he cannot use the power of government do the same within society. Locke recognizes the government's power to tax, but only for the purposes of underwriting the limited, negative powers of government. The power to tax is limited to those revenues necessary to protect those taxed against aggression. The taxing power can never be used to collect money from one individual or group in order to provide benefits to another. The individual's property must be *preserved*.

Furthermore, these limits would prohibit government from waging preemptive war. Since force may only be employed once a state of war exists between two parties, war may only be waged *after* one has committed an act of aggression against the other (and obviously only against the aggressor). Therefore, the government may not initiate war. It may only employ its military force to *defend* the individuals it governs.

Locke on the form of government

Having established the powers vested in government and their limits, Locke goes on to establish the form of government that will best exercise those powers for the good of the people. Before even describing his own vision, he eliminates any doubt that he disagrees with Hobbes.

"Hence it is evident, that absolute monarchy, which by some men is counted the only government in the world, is indeed inconsistent with civil society, and so can be no form of civil-government at all:"[17]

For Locke, not only must the power of the government be limited, rather than absolute, but it must be divided. Like Rousseau, Locke argues that the legislative power must be separated from the executive power, with the legislative supreme over the executive. This ensures that those who make the laws are not able to execute them themselves, which would be a conflict of interest. Having exercised the power to make the laws, the legislators are then subject to those laws themselves, which are executed by another branch of government.

For Locke, the legislative power of government should be vested in an assembly that is elected by majority vote of the whole people. It is in this way that the people give their consent to the laws the legislative body passes and thus all acts of government, which are all subordinate to those laws. The executive power is subordinate to the legislative. It merely "executes" the laws passed by the legislature, rather than exercises any independent power of its own.

On the surface, Rousseau and Locke seem here to agree, raising the concern both would have society subject to the "tyranny of the majority." However, for Locke, although the legislative power is supreme over the executive power, it is limited in the power it can wield in legislating. It can only enforce the non-aggression principle. Therefore, it may only make laws consistent with this principle, lest it become an aggressor itself.

This is a crucial difference between Rousseau and Locke. Rousseau grants absolute power to the majority, while Locke limits that power. By exceeding those limits on its power, even a democratically-elected government destroys those rights it exists to protect. Locke calls the idea that anyone would consent to such a government "too gross an absurdity for any man to own."[18]

So to those liberals who reply "That's why we have elections" to any suggestion that the government has overstepped its bounds, Locke says, "No, government doesn't have that power, *regardless of the wishes of the majority.*"

A majority is just a collection of individuals. If no one individual has the power to force someone else to purchase health insurance, for example, then the majority can't have that power, either. It violates the law of nature, which says every person has the liberty to dispose of his own possessions as he sees fit.

In order to ensure the legislative power stays within these natural limits, Locke has further rules which both the legislative and executive power must obey.

"And so whoever has the legislative or supreme power of any commonwealth, is bound to govern by established standing laws, promulgated and known to the people, and not by extemporary decrees; by indifferent and upright judges, who are to decide controversies by those laws; and to employ the force of the community at home, only in the execution of such laws, or abroad to prevent or redress foreign injuries, and secure the community from inroads and invasion. And this to be directed to no other end, but the peace, safety, and public good of the people."[19]

Locke on the right of revolution

Having established the powers of government and its form, Locke goes on to describe the way in which political societies are dissolved or destroyed. Here again, Locke's departs from both Hobbes and Rousseau.

Hobbes asserted that political society is destroyed when the power of the sovereign is divided or diminished in any way. Rousseau argued that the dissolution of government occurred when the executive power ceased to conform to the general will, embodied in the legislative power. While Locke agrees the executive can pose this danger, he goes a step further. Locke says even the will of the majority can be a danger to society.

"First, the legislative acts against the trust reposed in them, when they endeavor to invade the property of the subject, and to make themselves, or any part of the community, masters, or arbitrary disposers of the lives, liberties, or fortunes of the people."[20]

When the legislative branch of government goes beyond the rightful limits of its power, it actually destroys the society it is instituted to protect. It is at this point that Locke introduces a truly "revolutionary" idea, one which should be familiar to all Americans.

"The reason why men enter into society, is the preservation of their property; and the end why they chuse and authorize a legislative, is, that there may be laws made, and rules set, as guards and fences to the properties of all the members of the society, to limit the power, and moderate the dominion, of every part and member of the society: for since it can never be supposed to be the will of the society, that the legislative should have a power to destroy that which every one designs to secure, by entering into society, and for which the people submitted themselves to legislators of their own making; whenever the legislators endeavour to take away, and destroy the property of the people, or to reduce them to slavery under arbitrary power, they put themselves into a state of war with the people, who are thereupon absolved from any farther obedience, and are left to the common refuge, which God hath provided for all men, against force and violence. *Whensoever therefore the legislative shall transgress this fundamental rule of society; and either by ambition, fear, folly or corruption, endeavour to grasp themselves, or put into the hands of any other, an absolute power over the lives, liberties, and estates of the people; by this breach of trust they forfeit the power the people had put into their hands for quite contrary ends, and it devolves to the people, who have a right to resume their original liberty, and, by the establishment of a new legislative, (such as they shall think fit) provide for their own safety and security, which is the end for which they are in society.*"[21] [emphasis added]

This right of revolution, the right of the people to dissolve any government which violates their rights rather than protects them, was the principle upon which the founding fathers justified the American Revolution. Consider the similarity of the above passage to the one below.

"That whenever any Form of Government becomes destructive of these ends, it is the Right of the People to alter or to abolish it, and to institute new Government, laying its foundation on such principles and organizing its powers in such form, as to them shall seem most likely to effect their Safety and Happiness."[22]

Locke on economic policy

As his essay is a philosophical work, Locke does not develop a detailed economic theory like those you might expect from a modern think tank. But Locke's ideas directly influenced Adam Smith. In his famous *Wealth of Nations*, Smith wrote,

"All systems, either of preference or of restraint, therefore, being thus completely taken away, the obvious and simple *system of natural liberty* establishes itself of its own accord. Every man, as long *as he does not violate the laws of justice*, is left perfectly free to pursue his own interests his own way, and to bring both his industry and capital into competition with those of other men."[23]

It's impossible not to recognize Locke's stamp on this passage. It's his natural rights and non-aggression theory applied to economics. The general rule of economic activity is "natural liberty." The only restraint upon economic actors should be the "laws of justice," which is just another name for Locke's "law of nature." As Jefferson said, this is all from which the law should restrain anyone. For Smith, economic matters are no different. When you take away the arbitrary controls both liberals and conservatives would place on economic activity and allow economic actors to exercise their natural right to liberty, you are left with what we today call *a free market*.

Ironically, Smith's famous free market treatise was not written against liberals, but conservatives. Smith's purpose was to refute the conservative mercantilist system that we've seen Burke and Kirk so staunchly defend. But it goes without saying that it also condemns the liberal economic system, whether democratic or socialist.

Any system which violates the natural right to acquire property and *dispose of it as one sees fit*, as Locke would put it, is inconsistent with the laws of nature, the natural rights and the true purpose of government.

This is why you there was no regulatory state in early America as we know it today. There was no Securities Exchange Commission, Federal Trade Commission, Social Security, or Public Works Administration. "New Deal" might sound great, until you consider that the "Old Deal" was natural liberty and the American Creed. You can't have both, because the New Deal destroys the Old.

Conservatives and liberals now defend the New Deal as necessary to end the Great Depression and "save capitalism from itself," but this is just the same obfuscation that apologists for government intervention say about everything. At the time, the New Deal was fiercely opposed by proponents of the free market, who today make a very good case that it actually prolonged the Depression rather than ended it.

Liberals say the free market leaves those of lesser ability or plain bad luck without any means of support, but this bears no resemblance to reality. We have plenty of photographs of 19th century America, before massive government programs were established to fight poverty. We don't see poor people dying in the streets. That's because in the absence of government programs, myriad voluntary associations existed that actually did a much better job. The extent to which Americans formed voluntary associations to address social concerns astonished de Tocqueville:

"Americans of all ages, all conditions, and all dispositions, constantly form associations. They have not only commercial and manufacturing companies, in which all take part, but associations of a thousand other kinds – religious, moral, serious, futile, extensive, or restricted, enormous or diminutive. The Americans make associations to give entertainments, to found establishments for education, to build inns, to construct churches, to diffuse books, to send missionaries to the antipodes; and in this manner they found hospitals, prisons, and schools."[24]

Refuting every liberal and conservative economic argument against free markets is beyond the scope of this book. What is important to take away is the inherent conflict between both the conservative and liberal economic systems and the philosophical basis for the American Creed. You can't have mercantilism, socialism or Rousseau's democratic economic system and retain the inalienable rights to life, liberty and the pursuit of happiness at the same time. You have to choose.

Locke on foreign policy

As with economic policy, Locke's foreign policy has to be inferred from his general principles, but that isn't difficult either. Locke applies the same law of non-aggression to governments as he applies to individuals:

"Should a robber break into my house, and with a dagger at my throat make me seal deeds to convey my estate to him, would this give him any title? Just such a title, by his sword, has an unjust conqueror, who forces me into submission. The injury and the crime is equal, whether committed by the wearer of a crown, or some petty villain."[25]

Just as the government has no right to forcibly intervene against individuals, unless an individual has committed aggression against one of its citizens, so the government cannot make war against another nation unless it has committed an act of war against its citizens as a whole.

A foreign policy based on non-aggression is implicit in the declaration of war power in the Constitution. It is not the power to initiate a war, but to *declare* one. In other words, it is a power to formally recognize something that already exists, because of the aggressive actions of the opponent.

The language of every declaration of war by Congress in U.S. history supports this. Each one has three basic elements: to name the acts of war committed by the other nation; to recognize the existence of the war; to direct the president to use the military forces to end the war, not start it. For example, in declaring war on Mexico, Congress resolved,

"Whereas, *by the act of the Republic of Mexico*, a state of war *exists* between that Government and the United States: Be it enacted by the Senate and House of Representatives of the United States of American in Congress assembled, That for the purpose of enabling the government of the United States *to prosecute said war to a speedy and successful termination,* the President be, and he is hereby authorized to employ the militia, naval, and military forces of the United States,...[26]

Somehow, the requirement that the other nation commit an overt act of war before the United States employs military force has been totally lost. Now, both liberals and conservatives talk about going to war as long as "vital national interests" are involved. But vital national interests might be involved even if no act of aggression has been committed by anyone. In those cases, war isn't justified, at least as far as the non-aggression principle is concerned.

It's not a coincidence that American foreign policy was one of non-intervention for more than a century after the founding. It was not until the old philosophy, the one which underpins the American Creed, was abandoned that America began getting involved in wars with nations that had not previously attacked it.

Obviously, the "Bush Doctrine" of preemptive war completely contradicts this principle. But it didn't really start with Bush. There is at least one reason the United States didn't declare war on Korea, Viet Nam, Somalia, Iraq or the dozens of other countries it has been involved militarily in: it couldn't. With no *acts of war* committed by those nations against the United States, there was no *state of war* to declare.

Just like proponents for government intervention into the economy, proponents for America's interventionist foreign policy have a hundred reasons why preemptive war is necessary. Just like in economics, there are also hundreds of books you can read about why it's not.

But it comes down to this. You can't have preemptive war and the American Creed. Just like with economic policy, you have to choose.

Conclusion

The American Creed is actually a succinct summary of Locke's entire philosophy. It states that man's equality and natural rights are "self-evident," just as Locke did. It asserts that the purpose of government is to "secure these rights," not to take them away or to replace them with government-granted privileges. Finally, it states that when the government becomes "destructive of these ends," that the people have a right to dissolve the government and form a new one.

Locke's ideas are probably more radical now than they were when he wrote them down in the late 17th century. Today, the idea that the power of the government must be limited, *even when exercising the will of the majority*, is completely absent from modern American political discourse.

Americans today generally believe that once a representative is democratically elected, there are no limits to the power he can exercise. Neither do they recognize any limits to the power of the president once he has won the presidential election.

Yet, it was Locke's philosophy of limited government power that clearly inspired the Declaration of Independence. The Declaration's famous preamble states, consistent with Locke and in refutation of Hobbes, Burke and Rousseau, that the natural rights are *inalienable*. It makes the unqualified statement that the purpose of government is "to secure these rights." It is not to dominate every natural human impulse, nor to impose economic equality.

It was Locke's philosophy that defined the word "liberty" as it was understood by the signers. It is Locke's ideas, championed later by Thomas Jefferson and his Republicans, which most Americans think of when they reflect on what freedom really means.

At different times, the men who advanced these ideas called themselves by different names, including Whigs, Patriots and Republicans. Retrospectively, they are often called "classical liberals," in order to distinguish them from modern liberals, whose philosophy bears no resemblance to their own.

For our purposes, we will call them by the name they would be called in our century, based upon their philosophical and political beliefs.

The founding fathers were libertarians.

Chapter Five:

Defending the Creed: The Conservative Tide

"Sometimes it is said that man can not be trusted with the government of himself. Can he, then, be trusted with the government of others?"

– Thomas Jefferson 1st Inaugural Address (March 4, 1801)

Are you still there?

If so, congratulations! You've just covered arguably the entire gamut of political philosophy relevant to 21st century American politics. Of course, there are hundreds of other important writers and thinkers in all of the traditions we've looked at, but what we've tried to provide are the best and most comprehensive arguments for three ways of looking at organizing society: rule by the few, rule by the many, and individual self-rule.

If this little book accomplishes nothing else, I hope it inspires you to read Hobbes, Locke, Rousseau, Burke and even Marx extensively. Ideas matter!

Let's be honest. If you asked ten friends to spend the evening with you discussing dusty old books written by philosophers who lived hundreds of years ago, you probably wouldn't expect to need too many chairs. If you said you wanted to discuss two centuries of American history, you probably wouldn't need too many more. That's because our way of looking at studying history couldn't be more counterproductive.

Most people think of history as a very dry discipline concerned with memorizing names, events and dates that for some reason are supposed to be significant in shaping the world we live in. That's one way to approach it, but it isn't much fun. We're going to take a different approach.

We're going to look at the last two hundred and forty or so years in the context of the ideas we've learned about, including our central idea: the American Creed. American history can very much be seen as life, liberty and the pursuit of happiness struggling to break free of the ideological chains that have bound them for most of human history. American history is full of ebbs and flows, with the Creed dominating American life at some times and holding on for dear life at others.

Before we "get down to it," there are a few disclaimers we should get out of the way.

First, we need to recognize the need to over-generalize a bit. When we talk about people being "conservatives" or "liberals" or "libertarians," we mean that they seemed most influenced by those schools of thought.

Nobody is one hundred percent consistent. Human beings are imperfect, inconsistent creatures.

For example, Thomas Jefferson was mostly libertarian. A good argument can be made that he is the "founding father" of libertarianism in America. But when it came to education, he was completely *unlibertarian*. He devoted much of his life to promoting public education, for all of the same reasons Hobbes and Rousseau said education should be provided by the government: to indoctrinate students into the right way of thinking.

Ironically, Jefferson wanted to indoctrinate students to think like libertarians, which is why he proposed that resolution to the Board of Governors of the University of Virginia in the prologue to our last chapter. He didn't want to make attending school compulsory, but subsidization would be, as all tax subsidies are. One can't help imagining a Monty Python sketch: "I *order* you to be free!"

John Adams is another example. Virtually every significant policy he proposed was consistent with Burkean constitutional conservatism. When push came to shove in the early American republic, he sided with the Hobbesian centralists as the lesser of two evils over Jefferson and the libertarians. He based most of his positions on his rejection of the idea that all men are created equal. He just didn't believe that, not even in the limited sense of political equality as the Creed defines it.

But he did profess to believe in inalienable rights, even though their existence depends upon the assumption that we *are* created equal. Few have expressed the idea of inalienable rights more eloquently:

"I say RIGHTS, for such they have, undoubtedly, antecedent to all earthly government, — Rights, *that cannot be repealed or restrained by human laws* — Rights, derived from the great Legislator of the universe."[1]

How do we resolve this? It's simple. Even very brilliant people can be wrong about some things. John Adams was no dummy. Neither were Thomas Hobbes, John Locke nor Jean-Jacques Rousseau. All of these were very brilliant men, admittedly a lot smarter than your humble author. But they can't all be right.

It's fashionable today to reject "extremism" out of hand on any subject. The Hegelian proposition that the "truth is the synthesis of the extremes" is universally accepted and anyone who says "always" or "absolutely" is written off as an extremist or uncompromising.

But some things are absolutely true. $2+2 = 4$ is absolutely true. There are no extreme opinions about it that have to be synthesized to find that truth. There is one answer. All others are wrong.

This can just as easily be applied to the world of ideas, even political ideas. Whichever proposition is correct, rights are either inalienable or alienable. They can't be both. We are either all created equal in terms of any inherent authority we might possess over others or we're unequal. It is *impossible* for both to be true.

So, you really have to decide who you thought was right or wrong among the philosophers we've looked at in previous chapters. It's tempting to use Hegelian logic and say they were all right to a degree or all wrong to a degree. But it just doesn't work.

Right here in the real world, we are faced daily with the choice of recognizing that our fellow human beings have an inalienable right to liberty or they don't. There is no room for compromise. Once you compromise an inalienable right, it's no longer a right. At best, it's a privilege. There is just no way around that.

What will come as a surprise as we look at American history is how relevant the writings of Hobbes, Locke, Rousseau, Burke and Marx are to what actually happened in the real world of American history. Over and over, we'll hear political leaders paraphrasing their ideas and putting their ideas into practice. Virtually every significant event or movement in American history is deeply rooted in one of the philosophies we've looked at.

American society in the 21st century is quite literally the result of the decisions made by previous Americans to accept or reject the American Creed at different times and in response to different events.

That leads us into one last disclaimer. While we don't want to look at history as a sterile list of names, dates and events, we don't want to look at it as a battle of good vs. evil, either. Politics inspires a lot of passion in people, regardless of their philosophical bent. It is easy to paint the people we agree with as good and those we disagree with as evil.

But "evil" is a very strong word. When used to describe people, it means that people intentionally do what they know to be wrong. If we've learned anything from studying the philosophers who influence the various political schools of thought, that's just not true. Thomas Hobbes *believed* what he wrote was true and that his recommendations for organizing society were what would lead to the most human happiness. So did Locke. So did Rousseau, Burke and Marx.

We all have friends we disagree with on politics. Most of my friends disagree with me. That doesn't make them evil people. On the contrary, my friends are some of the best people who have ever lived, in my opinion. That's why I'm honored to be friends with them. I just believe they're wrong about certain things. But I don't believe they intentionally want to hurt people.

Certainly, there is corruption in politics. Wherever that much power and money is concentrated into one place, there is constant temptation for one's self-interest to overcome his willingness to do the right thing. But even if you could put the politician guilty of corruption on a truth serum, virtually none would say they intentionally did the wrong thing.

Human beings have a peculiar ability to rationalize their failings as benevolent acts. The politician who accepted a bribe or participated in a quid pro quo would find a reason why, despite the obvious conflict of interest, his behavior actually benefitted his constituents. This is something we all do; we deceive ourselves into thinking we're more virtuous than we are. Adam Smith talked about that hundreds of years ago, too:

"This self-deceit, this fatal weakness of mankind, is the source of half the disorders of human life. If we saw ourselves in the light in which others see us, or in which they would see us if they knew at all, a reformation would generally be unavoidable. We could not otherwise endure the sight."[2]

So, let's remember our mission here in looking at American history. We're not trying to find good guys or bad guys. We're trying to determine what philosophical perspectives were influencing the actors of history and how consistent their thinking was with the American Creed.

With all of that said, as Marty Dibergi of *Spinal Tap* fame would say, "Enough of my yacking. Whaddya say? Let's boogie!"

Colonial America

We've defined the founding of the American republic as having occurred in 1776, but the American story begins a century and a half before. European settlements existed even earlier, but the socio-political system that became the United States of America grew specifically out of the British colonies. The first two permanent colonies were in Jamestown (founded 1607) and Plymouth (1620).

Here is where we get a surprise. Unlike the mercantilist and fledgling free market economies of the later colonial period, these were both economically closer to something straight out of Karl Marx. Jamestown and Plymouth were both early modern experiments with communism. Both were microcosms for the larger disasters in communist countries of the 20th century.

Two centuries before Marx was born, the first "Americans" experimented with a quasi-voluntary communist system. I say "quasi-voluntary" because most of the settlers entered into a contract to share their property in common for a predetermined number of years. They weren't forced to do so by the British government. But once in America, they lived under the form of government defined in their charters and those governments did enforce a communist system.

In Plymouth, the "pilgrims" lost half of their number during the first winter. Replacements arrived in the spring, but the pilgrims lost half their number again the next winter. We all learned in kindergarten about the hardship the pilgrims faced early on.

What they never told us was *why* the pilgrims starved. Most of us were led to believe the pilgrims just didn't know how to grow food in the New

World. It wasn't until Squanto told them to plant a dead fish under every corn stalk that they learned to grow enough food to survive.

Squanto actually did teach them that trick, but that's not what saved them. Abandoning the communist system is what turned things around in Plymouth. We know this because the governor of the colony said so, explicitly. Here is what William Bradford said about why they starved:

"The experience that was had in this common course, and condition, tried sundry years, and that amongst godly, and sober men, may well evince, the vanity of that conceit, of Plato's, and other ancients, applauded by some of later times: that the taking away of property, and bringing in community, into, a commonwealth; would make them happy, and flourishing; as if they were wiser than God. For this community, (so far as it was) was found to breed much confusion, and discontent, and retard much employment, that would have been to their benefit, and comfort; for the young men that were most able and fit for labor and service, did repine that they should spend their time, and strength to work for other men's wives, and children, without any recompense. The strong, or man of parts, had no more in division of victuals, and clothes, than he that was weak, and not able to do a quarter the other could, this was thought *injustice*."[3]

Why was this injustice? Because it violated the law of nature "that no one should harm another in his life, health, liberty or possessions." If Locke was right, each colonist had a natural right to keep the fruits of his own labor and dispose of them as he saw fit. The communist system forcibly overrides this natural right and *the government* disposes of the fruits of each individual's labor as *it* sees fit.

Violating the natural law resulted in them starving, just as Locke would later say it would.

Bradford goes on to say that the wives considered it a form of slavery to have to cook and clean for men other than their husbands. Then, he makes a startling statement, considering these events also took place a century before Rousseau was born.

"Upon the point all being to have alike, and all to do alike, they thought themselves in the like condition, and one as good as another; and so if it did not cut off, those relations, that God hath set amongst men; yet it did at least much diminish, and take off, the mutual respects that should be preserved amongst them."[4]

What Bradford is talking about here is equality, but not the natural state of equality men are born in, where no one person has any inherent authority over another. It is Rousseau's *equality of results*, created by the government. The only way to achieve equality of results is to take away (i.e. "alienate") those natural rights the Creed says are inalienable. Rousseau told us this; he just didn't anticipate the results.

Neither did later communists in Russia, China, Viet Nam, Cambodia or other 20th century communist countries. They all had to learn the hard way, just as the pilgrims did. Their results were the same, but on a tragically much larger scale.

Bradford leaves no doubt about what turned things around for the pilgrims. As you may have surmised, it wasn't Squanto's trick with the dead fish:

"At length after much debate of things, the Governor (with the advice of the chiefest amongst them) gave way that they should set corn every man for his own particular, and in that regard trust to themselves; in all other things go on in the general way as before. And so assigned to every family a parcel of land, according to the proportion of their number, for that end, only for present use (but made no division for inheritance) and ranged all boys, and youth under some family. This had very good success; for it made all hands very industrious, so as much more corn was planted, than otherwise would have been; by any means the Governor or any other could use, and saved him a great deal of trouble, and gave far better content; the women now went willingly into the field, and took their little ones with them to set corn; which before would allege weakness and inability; whom to have compelled would have been thought great tyranny, and oppression."[5]

Wow. This paragraph is packed with information relevant to our investigation. First, Bradford's decision is to forsake the communist system for one of private property. The pilgrims each get "a parcel of land" for their own use. They weren't given total ownership because that was a stipulation of their contract with the investors, but they made land as close to being privately owned as their contract would allow.

What was the result? Everybody suddenly worked harder, because they were given the incentive to keep the fruits of their labor. In other words, their natural rights were restored and no longer overridden by the government. The women who felt enslaved under communism no longer felt that way, *even though they were working harder*.

Bradford also says that this private property system produced more corn than "any means the Governor or any other could use." In other words, the government can never come up with a plan that is going to be more productive than people working for themselves, on their own property, and keeping whatever they produce. Again, wow.

So, the very first lesson learned by the very first Americans was that private property, the right to keep the fruits of one's labor and dispose of them as one sees fit, is essential to life *and* liberty. They didn't learn this in a classroom or from some pie-in-the-sky philosopher. They learned it the hard way, trying to survive in a new world where no one was there to bail them out. When they tried communism, they starved. When they restored private property, they flourished and never starved again.

Every year, millions of children in public schools cut out crepe paper pilgrim hats and Native American headdresses during November. They decorate their classrooms with corn stalks and paper turkeys. They're told a story about the pilgrims that is completely the opposite of what really happened.

Without going into every detail, the experience in Jamestown was essentially identical. In fact, the lesson the pilgrims learned is a recurring theme in American history. Libertarian author Thomas Dilorenzo wrote a whole book about it, called *How Capitalism Saved America*. It documents government interventions into the economy in several periods of American history, whether conservative mercantilist or liberal democratic or socialist, and the disasters that inevitably resulted from each one. In every case, the restoration of property rights and "natural liberty" solved the problem and ended the crisis.

Dilorenzo's account of Jamestown also blows up another liberal myth:

"The Jamestown colonists had originally implored the Indians to sell them corn, but the Indians looked down on the settlers because they were barely capable of growing corn, thanks to their communistic economic system. After the introduction of private property and the resulting transformation, however, the Indians began coming to the colonists to acquire corn in return for furs and other items. That is, the colonists and the Indians began to engage in peaceful market exchange based on the division of labor. The mutual advantages of such a system are always conducive to peace as well as prosperity, as many of the colonists realized, for it makes little sense to make war on one's neighbor if one can prosper by trading."[6]

If 17th century Native Americans were at all an example of the "noble savage" Rousseau described and liberals like to characterize them as, their behavior bears no resemblance to what Rousseau described. They are not virtually unaware of their fellow creatures. They are discriminating, choosing not to engage in trade with the colonists when the colonists offered no value to them.

When the colonists adopt a private property system and begin to prosper, the natives completely change their stance. Contrary to Rousseau, they do indeed engage in the division of labor, free trade and voluntary contracts. They do so entirely out of self-interest, but by acting in their self-interest they also benefit the colonists, who do the same for the natives by acting in their own self-interest. They demonstrate Adam Smith's invisible hand in the real world, one hundred sixty years before Smith coined the phrase.

In other words, the first relationship between the English settlers in the first colony and the Native Americans who lived nearby was a free market relationship, based on property rights and voluntary trade to the mutual benefit of the traders. While this relationship lasted, it also fostered peace between the colonists and the natives.

Do you remember learning *that* in your public school history class?

Colonial America was in many ways a freer economy than any in history. Once they ended their experiments with communism, the Americans prospered to the point of astonishing British soldiers arriving in the New World to fight the French. The colonies were still part of the British Empire and its mercantilist economy, but they were to a large degree left alone by the British government.

That changed after the conflict we call the French and Indian War, called the Seven Years War in Europe. The British were victorious, but they had accumulated huge war debts in defeating the French. Taxpayers in Great Britain were bearing an enormous burden, while the colonists in America were paying almost no taxes to the crown. As we hear so often from our modern American media, "the government had to do something." It was more than just levy taxes.

Today, most Americans have no idea why their ancestors decided to secede from the British Empire. We're generally taught the whole conflict erupted over "taxation without representation." The British imposed taxes on the colonists without giving them representation in the British parliament and the colonists refused to comply. King George III sent troops to enforce the taxes and the American Revolution began.

Beyond taxation without representation

This hardly tells the whole story. While they did object to being taxed by a body they weren't represented in, the American colonists had no desire to be represented in the British Parliament. They made this explicit in the Declaration of Rights and Grievances of 1774:

"That it is inseparably essential to the freedom of a people, and the undoubted right of Englishmen, that no taxes be imposed on them but with their own consent, given personally, or by their representatives.

That the people of these colonies are not, and from their local circumstances cannot be, represented in the House of Commons, in Great Britain.

That the only representatives of the people of these colonies are persons chosen therein by themselves; and that no taxes have been, or ever can be constitutionally imposed on them but by their respective legislatures.

That all supplies to the Crown, being the free gifts of the people, *it is unreasonable and inconsistent with the principles and spirit of the British constitution for the people of Great Britain to grant His Majesty the property of the colonists.*"[7] [emphasis added]

The influence of Locke is explicit in the passage above, with the emphasis on property and the rejection of the idea that a simple majority vote legitimized the government's authority to tax the people.

Locke's influence is even more explicit in Samuel Adams' 1772 *Rights of the Colonists.*

"In short, it is the greatest absurdity to suppose it in the power of one, or any number of men, at the entering into society, to renounce their essential natural rights, or the means of preserving those rights; when the grand end of civil government, from the very nature of its institution, is for the support, protection, and defence of those very rights; the principal of which, as is before observed, are Life, Liberty, and Property. If men, through fear, fraud, or mistake, should in terms renounce or give up any essential natural right, the eternal law of reason and the grand end of society would absolutely vacate such renunciation. The right to freedom being the gift of God Almighty, it is not in the power of man to alienate this gift and voluntarily become a slave."[8]

Notice the similarities between this passage and the following passage in Locke's Second Treatise.

"Thirdly, the supreme power cannot take from any man part of his property without his own consent, for the preservation of property being the end of government, and that for which men enter into society, it necessarily supposes and requires, that the people should have property, without which they must be supposed to lose that, by entering society, which was the end for which they entered it; too gross an absurdity for any man to own."[9]

In today's vernacular, one might say Adams was "channeling Locke" in this piece. For Adams, the rights of life, liberty, and property are "inalienable." Considering Locke combined life, liberty, and justly acquired possessions into the general name "property," Adams is virtually quoting Locke directly.

Adams also draws an important clarification on inalienability from Locke. Not only can no human being or group of human beings take away the individual's natural rights, including by majority vote; *but an individual cannot even surrender his own* natural rights.

So, Adams provides yet another answer to "that's why we have elections." "No," says Adams, "that's not why we have them at all."

Regarding taxes, since the purpose of government is to *preserve* the natural rights, the government's power to tax is limited to collecting what is necessary to defend those rights. The government has no legitimate authority to collect taxes and spend the money for other purposes, especially to benefit people other than those taxed. While he's responding to the conservative British mercantilist scheme, the principle applies equally to liberal wealth redistribution.

Parliament vs. colonial assemblies

The British Empire in the 1770's was quintessential conservatism, much closer to Hobbes than Burke. The reasoning behind Parliament's claim that it could legislate for the colonies, even if the colonies were not represented, is straight out of Hobbes.

"The Romans, who had the sovereignty of many provinces, yet governed them always by presidents and praetors; and not by assemblies, as they governed the city of Rome and territories adjacent. In like manner, when there were colonies sent from England to plant Virginia, and Summer Islands, though the government of them here were committed to assemblies in London, yet did those assemblies never commit the government under them to any assembly there, but did to each plantation send one governor: for though every man, where he can be present by nature, desires to participate of government; yet where they cannot be present, they are by nature also inclined to commit the government of their common interest rather to a monarchical, than a popular, form of government..."[10]

Hobbes' remains consistent here with his indivisibility plank. Since the sovereign power cannot be divided, there is certainly no room for local legislatures in colonies making their own laws. Any assembly under the jurisdiction of the sovereign must merely advance the wishes of the sovereign, so the royally-appointed governors are a much more efficient and secure way of seeing that the sovereign power is not compromised.

Here was a conflict between British Hobbesian conservatism and American Lockean libertarianism and the way those ideas apply when the rubber hits the road in the real world. The separation from Great Britain was inevitable. You cannot have inalienable rights to life, liberty and property and Hobbesian conservatism at the same time.

Mercantilism vs. free trade

The colonists' objections were economic as well as political. They not only objected to what they saw as unconstitutional taxes and legislation, but also the economic motivation behind them. The colonists opposed the entire British mercantilist economic system, which sought to enrich the government and connected business interests at the colonists' expense.

Since all nations respond in kind to tariffs in a mercantilist system, the tariffs eventually cancel themselves out. Great Britain had no such problem with her colonies. Since she now claimed the authority to make laws and levy taxes on them, the colonies represented an opportunity for the British government to practice a purely one-sided form of mercantilism, where they could maneuver the colonies into buying purely British exports, regardless of the relative competitiveness of their prices.

This is incompatible with the colonists' Lockean view of inalienable rights to "dispose of his person and possessions as he sees fit." It also provoked Burkean conservatives who argued that they retained their prescriptive English liberties, violated by the "innovative" new taxes.

Following classic mercantilist policy, the British granted a monopoly on importing tea to the East India Tea Company. Outright monopolies were the original method for creating the small group of privately held corporations that comprise the "economic aristocracy" in the mercantilist system. They are dependent upon government privilege to maintain their position and reciprocally loyal to the government because of that dependency.

The real Boston Tea Party story

This is the backdrop for the real story behind the Boston Tea Party.

Rather than merely a protest against taxes levied without representation, the "destruction of the tea" was a reaction to repeated efforts by Parliament to control the colonial economy. In mercantilist fashion, Parliament had granted the East India Company a monopoly on importing tea into England. It paid a tax upon importation and then sold the tea to the public through resellers. It was not allowed to sell the tea retail.

By the time of the 1773 Tea Act, earlier controversies over taxation had already raged and subsided. The Tea Act did not impose new taxes on the colonies. Rather, it left an already existing tax on tea in place, but gave the East India Company two advantages. First, it reinstituted a refund of the import taxes the company paid in England. Second, it allowed the company to sell direct to the colonies, instead of having to export through resellers. The company would now sell direct to consignees in the colonies, hand-picked by the government.

This threatened both the "legitimate" colonial tea importers and also smugglers of Dutch Tea, as the tax-subsidized East India Company could now undercut them both. The colonists saw this as an attempt to bring the colonies under complete economic control. The British government was using its taxing power to eliminate all competition for its "crony capitalist" importer.

If successful, there was no reason to believe Parliament wouldn't follow suit with other goods the colonists imported. They foresaw a future where the British realized the mercantilist goal of completely controlling the colonial economy, benefitting the government and its connected business interests at colonial expense.

None of this struck the British as oppressive or even objectionable. In the conservative worldview, private property is a privilege granted by the government for the benefit of the commonwealth. The colonists should have been pleased with the great wealth the sovereign allowed them to keep and equally pleased they could serve the empire by participating in its mercantilist system.

There was only one problem. The colonists didn't see it that way. They saw it as Locke did, that the government's sole reason for existence was to *preserve* their property as individuals. This was the true root of the conflict.

Central Banking

Great Britain's central bank, the Bank of England, also played a part in the dispute. During the Seven Years War, the colonies had issued "bills of credit," which were paper currencies not backed by gold or any other commodity (a fiat currency), in order to help finance military expenses. As these paper notes circulated in the economy, they competed with the British pound sterling. As they were fiat currencies that were issued in greater volume than was eventually collected in taxes, their value tended to depreciate, harming British merchants who accepted them as payments.

As a result, the British passed laws in 1751 and 1764 restricting the ability of the colonies to issue their own currency. In fact, the British currency was actually more stable than the American currency, but that was not at issue. The British were now imposing their central bank's currency, which likewise represented an arbitrary power over the colonists in terms of controlling the value of the money the colonists were forced to use. As William Graham Sumner observed,

"In 1763 Parliament declared any colonial acts for issuing paper money void. Franklin wrote a pamphlet in opposition to this act. He said that gold and silver owe their value chiefly to the estimation in which they happen to be among the generality of nations and the credit given to the opinion that they will continue to be so held." [11]

Ironically, the British were doing the colonists a favor in overriding their desire to circulate paper currency. The colonists would later learn that the hard way with the Continental Dollar. But the Hobbesian tendency to centralize banking and the libertarian and constitutional conservative insistence on local control of the currency will be another recurring theme in American history.

Centralism vs. federalism

Burkean conservatives joined libertarians in opposing the British on constitutional grounds. For example, the tea tax had a constitutional aspect to it as well. In addition to advancing British mercantilism, the tea tax also underwrote the salaries of colonial judges, which rankled.

But there was a larger constitutional issue. The colonists recognized George III as their king, but believed the British Parliament had no legitimate power to legislate for the colonies outside of a very limited area.

Foreshadowing their later attempt to construct a federal government, the colonists believed that they retained most authority to govern and tax themselves. This idea that the central government should be limited and the bulk of the political power concentrated locally would also loom large throughout American history.

The role of government

So, it was much more than taxation without representation that led to the American Revolution. It was a fundamental philosophical difference between the colonists and the mother country about the relationship of the government to the governed and about the purpose of government.

The colonists believed that the government existed only to protect their rights and therefore could never violate them for the purposes of achieving collective goals. The government of Great Britain believed that the colonies were her property, which existed only to help the government achieve collective goals. Representation in the British parliament would not have resolved this dispute.

By 1776, the people of America were united as they would not be again at any time in their history. Following the anonymous publication of **Common Sense** by Thomas Paine, the thirteen colonies were resolved to one common purpose: to win their independence from Great Britain.

The dominant philosophy was Locke's. The preamble to the Declaration succinctly captured Locke's ideas about the self-evident equality of all mankind, the resulting existence of inalienable rights, and the government's sole purpose in "securing these rights." It paraphrases Locke in asserting that "That whenever any Form of Government becomes destructive of these ends, it is the Right of the People to alter or to abolish it, and to institute new Government, laying its foundation on such principles and organizing its powers in such form, as to them shall seem most likely to effect their Safety and Happiness."[12]

Implicit in these ideas is that whenever government, which is the societal use of force, undertakes anything other than protection of the inalienable rights, it must thereby violate those rights. The use of force for anything other than defense constitutes aggression. Such government action amounts to a violation of those rights it exists to protect.

Conservatives also supported the revolution, but for different reasons. For them, it was the king's sudden departure from long-established legal traditions and the resulting violation of prescriptive rights. Jefferson's Summary View had made both arguments, with the conservative argument for the colonists' "rights as Englishmen" more prevalent in that document. But the Declaration makes the case for revolution on a purely libertarian foundation.

The Declaration goes on to list the various ways in which King George III of England had failed to fulfill the purpose of government, the securing of natural rights. By violating those rights instead of securing them, he had become a tyrant, giving the colonists just cause to revoke his authority and set up their own government.

The libertarian federal republic

Having won their independence from Great Britain, the various colonies were now each independent states. Today, most Americans think of the word "state" to mean subdivision of the nation, considering New Hampshire, Texas, and California subdivisions of the nation known as "the United States of America."

However, when the Treaty of Paris was signed in 1783, no such distinction between the words "state" and "nation" existed. King George actually made a treaty wherein he recognized the independence of his former colonies as thirteen separate nations, each as independent from each other as France was from Spain or the Netherlands. This reality was reflected at the end of the Declaration of Independence, which did not assert the independence of a monolithic nation called "The United States of America," but rather:

"these United Colonies are, and of Right ought to be Free and Independent States; that they are Absolved from all Allegiance to the British Crown, and that all political connection between them and the State of Great Britain, is and ought to be totally dissolved; and that as Free and Independent States, they have full Power to levy War, conclude Peace, contract Alliances, establish Commerce, and to do all other Acts and Things which Independent States may of right do."[13]

Notice the word "they" is used in describing the powers now invested in these "independent states," rather than the word "it" in describing any monolithic entity, which is neither explicitly nor implicitly recognized. The colonies were "United Colonies" in their opposition to government by Great Britain, but were in all respects thirteen separate countries, each investing their governments with all of the power that the government of any sovereign nation would have.

That the States were all separate nations was also explicitly acknowledged in America's first form of "general government." Drafted in 1778 and ratified in 1783, the Articles of Confederation created the first government over the "united States of America." Under this written constitution, the recognition of the states as independent nations and the nature of their relationship to each other is made perfectly clear.

"Article I. The Stile of this Confederacy shall be "The United States of America."

Article II. Each state retains its sovereignty, freedom, and independence, and every Power, Jurisdiction, and right, which is not by this confederation expressly delegated to the United States, in Congress assembled.

Article III. The said States hereby severally enter into a firm league of friendship with each other, for their common defense, the security of their liberties, and their mutual and general welfare, binding themselves to assist each other, against all force offered to, or attacks made upon them, or any of them, on account of religion, sovereignty, trade, or any other pretense whatever."[14]

Notice the consistency with which the framers of the Articles applied Locke's principles of government. The separate states, or nations, delegate only limited powers to the federal government, retaining the rest for themselves. The purpose of the federal government is clearly stated: to defend the rights of the people of the states against aggression by some external force. The government must "secure" their rights, making clear that those rights existed before the government was formed. They are not created or granted by the government.

It also assumes the state governments possessed all power not reserved by the people before the Articles were adopted. Of these powers, they delegated certain of them to the federal government and kept the rest themselves. The states do not give up any power not delegated to the federal government, nor do the individuals in the states give up any power not originally delegated to the state governments. Individuals never give up *any* of their inalienable rights to either the state or federal governments.

That the various states formed a federal, rather than a national government, is clear from the language of the Articles. A federal government is the government of a federation, a union of equals agreeing to cooperate on certain objectives while retaining their independence and sovereignty. A national government assumes that the parties have given up their individual powers and delegated them all to a central government.

Both libertarians and constitutional conservatives had just fought together against the latter proposition. They constructed a new government that intentionally avoided any opportunity for power to centralize.

These ideas are likely completely foreign to most Americans. While we still refer to the government based in Washington, D.C. as "federal," it has become a national government in all but name. Sadly, most are not familiar with the idea that delegated power can be limited. Elections are largely seen as sanctions for whatever the winners may propose.

The best chance for 21st century Americans to understand federalism might come from science fiction. The Federation of Planets in Star Trek is much closer to the intent of the founders than the U.S. government.

This is a true federation, with a group of planets agreeing to delegate their mutual defense against the Klingons and Romulans to a federal government, while retaining all of the rest of their powers as well as their complete independence.

In the episode "Amok Time" from the original series, Kirk and McCoy visit Vulcan with Mr. Spock for his Vulcan marriage ceremony. There they are subject to Vulcan laws which are completely alien to them. Due to Kirk not understanding what he was agreeing to, he ends up having to fight Spock to the death!

The Vulcan law requiring mortal combat was considered completely barbaric by the Earth men, but there is no suggestion in the episode that it should be abolished or overridden by the Federation of Planets. That doesn't mean the other planets condone them, but rather recognize they have been delegated no power to change them.

Generalizations are essential in trying to impose some understandable order on a very diverse world. But is important to recognize that they are indeed generalizations. Both libertarians and conservatives often make the mistake of seeing early America as either a libertarian or conservative paradise, respectively. It was far from it.

It wasn't even purely a blend of libertarianism and Burkean conservatism. As Gutzman reminds us, "some states at the time of ratification [of the Constitution] had established state churches."[15] Considering that each state was its own nation, these were very Hobbesian centralist institutions, although admittedly some of these states were so small that wherever you traveled within them, you were still "local," even by 18th century standards.

Neither was the economy a purely free market. Adam Smith and Jean Baptiste Say had only written their treatises in 1776 and 1803, respectively. The idea of a free market was a very new one. But the natural tendency to apply Lockean libertarian principles to economic matters made the early American economy much freer than it otherwise would have been. Libertarians pushed for freer markets, while conservatives tended to oppose them.

So, differences began to emerge between libertarians and conservatives after the Revolutionary War was won and a common enemy no longer united them.

What was completely missing from early America was any influence of Rousseauian liberalism. Thomas Paine would later advocate what we might today call a "left libertarian" perspective in his Agrarian Justice and the second part of The Rights of Man. Historians disagree whether this was a later development following his long stay and political career in France or whether he indeed held those views when writing the more purely libertarian *Common Sense*. But Paine always maintained a natural right to all property other than land.

Regardless, it was libertarians and conservatives who dominated early American politics. For the first full century of American history, they fought some epic battles.

Hamilton and the Federalists

For that small percentage of Americans today that are even conscious of the first federal government, created by the Articles of Confederation; they have some recollection from a history class that it was "too weak" and was completely abolished by the U.S. Constitution. The independence of the states was revoked and they became "subdivisions" under "the supreme law of the land."

These are basically the arguments made by Alexander Hamilton for a much stronger central government than that created by the Articles. Hamilton's ideas came straight from the philosophy of Thomas Hobbes. As early as 1780, before the revolution was won or the Articles were even officially ratified, Hamilton was making arguments that will by now seem familiar.

"The fundamental defect *is a want of power in Congress*. It is hardly worth while to show in what this consists, as it seems to be universally acknowledged, or to point out how it has happened, as the only question is how to remedy it. It may however be said that it has originated from three causes – an excess of the spirit of liberty, which has made the particular states show a jealousy of all power not in their own hands; and this jealousy has led them to exercise a right of judging in the last resort of the measures recommended by Congress, and of acting according to their own opinions of their propriety or necessity, a diffidence in Congress of their own powers, by which they have been timid and indecisive in their resolutions, constantly making concessions to the states, till they have scarcely left themselves the shadow of power; a want of sufficient means at their disposal to answer the public exigencies and of vigor to draw forth those means; which have occasioned them to depend on the states individually to fulfill their engagements with the army, and the consequence of which has been to ruin their influence and credit with the army, to establish its dependency on each state separately rather than *on them*, that is rather than on the whole collectively."[16] [emphasis added]

Clearly, Hamilton was hostile toward the federal system, wherein the states reserved most powers to themselves and only delegated limited powers to the central government. What is the impending result of this "want of power' in the central government? Like Hobbes, Hamilton concludes that the absence of centralized power inevitably leads to civil war.

"…a little time hence, some of the states will be powerful empires, and we are so remote from other nations that we shall have all the leisure and opportunity we can wish to cut each other's throats."[17]

As Robin might have said to Batman, "Holy Hobbes!"

Like Hobbes, Hamilton believed all commonwealths are de facto enemies of one another, as they have no common sovereign "keeping them in awe" and thus preventing them from harming one another. As the states were created as separate, independent nations, Hamilton saw them no differently than the warring nations of Europe.

For Hamilton, the states keeping their sovereignty was doomed to failure. Only a single collective, dominated by the absolute power of a central sovereign, could endure peacefully. The longer the several states retained their independence and the central government suffered from "a want of power," the more imminent the danger of unavoidable civil war.

Neither did Hamilton view individuals differently than Hobbes. In a November 1775 letter to John Jay, Hamilton expresses his concern over a raid into New York to shut down a loyalist newspaper. While Hamilton shares the perpetrators' contempt for the content of the newspaper, he is more concerned about the lack of control by a central authority over the various colonies. His comments on the incident include his view of human nature:

133

"In times of such commotion as the present, while the passions of men are worked up to an uncommon pitch there is great danger of fatal extremes. The same state of the passions which fits the multitude, who have not a sufficient stock of reason and knowledge to guide them, for opposition to tyranny and oppression, very naturally leads them to a contempt and disregard of all authority. The due medium is hardly to be found among the more intelligent, it is almost impossible among the unthinking populace. When the minds of these are loosened from their attachment to ancient establishments and courses, they seem to grow giddy and are apt more or less to run into anarchy."[18]

One could not ask for a more Hobbesian view of the nature of man.

This was the period after the battles of Lexington and Concord and before the Declaration of Independence. The Americans had laid siege to Boston, where the British troops were garrisoned. The British had not yet invaded New York City. There was no central authority over the American colonies at all, other than the Continental Congress.

A situation such as this would have horrified Hobbes. It certainly did Hamilton.

Hamilton assumes that the majority of people are "unthinking," ruled by their passions rather than their reason. He argues that when the dominating power of the sovereign is taken away (attachment to ancient establishments), the natural result will be that the people will "grow giddy and run into anarchy."

Throughout the war for independence and for the entire period between the Treaty of Paris and the Constitutional Convention, Hamilton made the same arguments for a more powerful central government. It was future members of his Federalist Party that pushed for and finally succeeded in seating a convention to rework the Articles of Confederation.

But Hamilton himself had no intention of merely refining what he saw as a completely flawed system. Hamilton wished to scrap the Articles of Confederation and replace them with a completely different form of government. Most Americans today would be shocked at its form. According to James Madison's notes on the Constitutional Convention, this is what Hamilton proposed:

"In his private opinion he had no scruple in declaring, supported as he was by the opinions of so many of the wise & good, that the British Govt. was the best in the world: and that he doubted that anything short of it would do in American."[19]

This was by no means a misunderstanding on Madison's part. In a letter to George Washington only a few weeks after his speech at the convention, Hamilton was pleased to report,

"A plain but sensible man, in a conversation I had with him yesterday, expressed himself nearly in this manner. The people begin to be convinced that their "excellent form of government" as they have been used to call it, will not answer their purpose; and that they must substitute something not very remote from that which they have lately quitted."[20]

Hamilton would not express these ideas publicly due to the public's complete abhorrence of monarchy. The Constitutional Convention itself was not open to the public and the notes taken by Madison and Robert Yates were not published until decades after it had adjourned. In this protected setting, Hamilton felt comfortable in laying out his true agenda.

It was completely opposite of views he later expressed in the Federalist essays.

The centralizers' plan

Hamilton did stop short of calling for an actual monarchy, but his "Plan of Government" was a constitutional monarchy in all but name. His notes on this plan survive:

1. The executive power would be invested in a "Governor," who would be elected *for life*. His proposal granted the Governor all of the powers eventually granted to the President of the United States under the Constitution.

2. The legislative power would be invested in two bodies, an Assembly elected by the people for three year terms, and a senate elected by the people *for life*. In addition to the powers granted to the Senate under the Constitution, Hamilton would have bestowed the power to declare war on the Senate alone, rather than on the whole Congress, including the Assembly.

3. The general government would appoint the state governors and would have a negative on all laws passed within the several states.[21]

According to Robert Yates, Hamilton felt it necessary to explain to the convention why this form of government was *not* a monarchy.

"It may be said, this constitutes an elective monarchy? Pray, what is a monarchy? May not the governors of the respective states be considered in that light? But by making the executive subject to impeachment, the term monarchy cannot apply."[22]

It would seem that Hamilton truly had studied his Hobbes, who said the sovereign power was inalienable. That this is the only distinction that Hamilton draws between his form of government and a monarchy is perhaps more compelling than any other evidence of his Hobbesian outlook.

Hamilton's plan was as close to the British monarchy as he believed he could get away with in the anti-monarchical environment of 1787 America. His executive had a different name and was elected by the people, but for life. The senate under Hamilton's plan would mirror the House of Lords, while the Assembly would mirror the House of Commons. Like the British monarchy, the governors of the *provinces*, which is how Hamilton viewed the states, were to be appointed by the central government. The declaration of war power was also reserved to the Senate, the portion of Congress elected for life, rather than the Assembly, which was chosen by the people in frequent elections.

Overall, Hamilton's plan attempted to concentrate power into one man, supported by a privileged elite, all with lifetime positions in the government. But the most Hobbesian aspect of Hamilton's plan was not how the power was distributed, but the extent of the power he wished to grant. Hamilton specified that the legislature of the United States would be invested "with power to pass all *laws whatsoever*, subject to the *negative* hereafter mentioned."[23] [emphasis in the original] In other words, contrary to America's founding principles, there was to be no limits on the power of the national government.

That this absolute power would be invested in the legislature might seem Rousseauian on the surface. However, on this point, there is very little difference between Hobbes and Rousseau. Both invested absolute power in the sovereign and Hobbes repeatedly conceded that the sovereign might be an assembly. The stark difference between Hobbes and Rousseau were their respective ideas about the *purpose* of government. As we have seen, Hamilton is completely Hobbesian on this.

While Hamilton was arguably the purest Hobbesian at the convention, he was certainly not alone in wanting more centralized power. Despite their later antagonism, James Madison had ideas very similar to Hamilton's. He shared Hamilton's desire to establish a national government, rather than a federal one. Madison himself repeatedly proposed a Congressional veto over state laws throughout the convention, which was consistently voted down. His proposal for Congressional power to charter corporations to build interstate canals was similarly rejected. Madison's most substantive proposals were so thoroughly rejected that biographer Kevin Gutzman quipped,

"Far from being the 'father of the Constitution,' then, Madison was an unhappy witness to its C-section birth. Perhaps he would more appropriately be called an attending nurse. He certainly did not think of it as his own offspring."[24]

The difference between Madison and Hamilton was their respective reactions to the results of the convention. Madison acquiesced to the verdict of the delegates and recognized they had rejected a national government. Hamilton would not accept the results and continued to attempt to mold the federal government into a national one. For the rest of his political career, Hamilton set out to subvert the limits on power embodied in the Constitution and concentrate more and more power in the central government.

A new republic

The first government formed under the new Constitution was almost as revolutionary as the one formed in 1776. With Hamilton as treasury secretary, the new government set out to mimic the British Empire from which it had previously won its independence.

In terms of economic and foreign policy, Hamilton laid the foundation for America conservatism. While conservative politicians may invoke Jeffersonian free markets and limited government in their rhetoric, *in practice* they have consistently promoted mercantilism, a large standing military force, and an aggressive foreign policy. It was these conservative policies that Jefferson and his Republicans of the late 18th century opposed, based upon their Lockean philosophy of government limited to defending life, liberty, and property.

Religious freedom?

Religion, too, was as central to conservative thinking in the 18th century as it is today. While Jefferson was writing Virginia's Statue on Religious Freedom, hoping to build a "wall of separation" between church and state, Federalist John Adams was drafting the Massachusetts State Constitution, which empowered the state to force its citizens to attend religious instruction.[25]

Despite their later disagreements, Adams agreed with Hamilton in wanting to recreate the British system of government in America. Hamilton's emphasis was economic; Adams' social and religious. Both proceeded from the same conservative worldview.

Like Hamilton and Madison, Adams feared what he saw as the tendency towards mob rule under republican government, and so believed it was imperative that the government not only defend its citizens' rights, but promote virtue as well. This ancient conservative idea runs contrary to Locke's non-aggression principle. By definition, the *promotion* of anything by government represents the initiation of force.

Adams and Hamilton ultimately disagreed on particulars, not philosophy. Adams' conservatism was certainly more Burkean, meaning he viewed the nature of man and the role of government as Hamilton did, but didn't always agree on the best means towards its ends.

The seeds of militarism

On a large military establishment in peacetime, Adams opposed Hamilton's push for a standing army, but did support a large navy. He believed the "wooden walls" of a formidable navy would add to the republic's negotiating strength, even when seeking to avoid war. He feared Hamilton's plans to raise a large standing army with which Hamilton could expand the "American empire," not on principle, but on his estimation of its prudence.

A century later, American expansion would begin just as Hamilton envisioned it, by way of war with Spain.

The return of mercantilism

Regarding Hamilton's economic agenda, Adams gave it passive support. As David McCullough observes, Adams had always "candidly admitted his ignorance of coin and commerce."[26] While most modern politicians may be similarly ignorant of the significance of the economic policy they enact, most do not have the personal integrity to admit it as Adams did.

Thus, Adams did not object to the formation of the Bank of the United States, the nation's first central bank. Hamilton had lobbied hard to establish it, further emulating the mercantilist economic system of Great Britain, which had established its own central bank in 1694. Jefferson fought hard against it, seeing it as a key plank in giving control over the economy to the federal government.

There were other tenets of Hamilton's platform that Adams agreed with more actively. He did believe in titles of nobility, although not hereditary ones. As McCullough also points out,

"Like Richard Henry Lee, Adams believed the need for "distinctions" ran deep in human nature and that to deny this was unrealistic. The love of titles was like the love of parades and pageantry. The title did not make the man, of course, but it enhanced the standing of the man in the eyes of others. Rank and distinction were essential to any social organization, be it a family, a parish, or a ship, Adams would say."[27]

This affectation of Adams' grew out of his conservative belief that a "natural aristocracy" of talented men would help guide the nation towards virtue and restrain the animal impulses that egalitarianism encouraged. This view is consistent throughout conservative thought, from Hobbes to Burke to Adams to Kirk.

Hobbesians and Burkeans unite on absolute power

The most important philosophical agreement between Adams and Hamilton concerned the power invested in the government. For Adams, as for Hobbes, Burke and Hamilton, the power invested in the government must be absolute. Like Burke, he may have believed it should be divided, while Hobbes and Hamilton believed it should not, but all four believed the individual gave up all power to the government somewhere. For Burke and Adams, if any power was withheld from the executive or central government, the balance resided in the legislature or local government, respectively. None was retained by the individual.

This is implicit in all of Adams' writings, including his ***Defence of the Constitutions of the United States of America***. While he argues for the importance of the separation and proper balance of powers between the legislative, the executive, and the judiciary, even for balancing legislative power between democratic and aristocratic assemblies; his reasoning consistently assumes that *the total power resides somewhere in the government*.

If you saw the superb mini-series on John Adams based on McCullough's biography, the Adam's character, played by Paul Giamatti, perfectly sums up Adams' differences with Jefferson on this point:

"Doctor, Mr. Jefferson's pet topic is not the artful arrangement of political power, but the cordoning off of a space in which no power exists at all."[28]

Whether Adams ever really said that or not, it not only perfectly captures Adams' and Jefferson's personal differences, but the differences between libertarians and conservatives in general. Libertarians believe that most areas of life are completely beyond the reach of the government. The government's only power is to respond to aggression. Absent aggression, the government is literally powerless against the individual.

Conservatives don't believe that. They believe the government is all-powerful. Hobbesians like Hamilton wish to centralize that power on one place, while Burkean conservatives like Adams which to "artfully arrange it" in checks and balances, but both leave none to the individual.

Jefferson expressed the libertarian position repeatedly throughout his life. In an 1816 letter to Francis Walker Gilmer, he wrote,

"Our legislators are not sufficiently apprised of the rightful limits of their powers; that their true office is to declare and enforce only our natural rights and duties, and to take none of them from us. No man has a natural right to commit aggression on the equal rights of another; and this is all from which the laws ought to restrain him."[29]

On government enforcement of religious beliefs or practices, he said,

"The error seems not sufficiently eradicated, that the operations of the mind, as well as the acts of the body, are subject to the coercion of the laws. But our rulers can have authority over such natural rights only as we have submitted to them. The rights of conscience we never submitted, *we could not submit*. We are answerable for them to our God. *The legitimate powers of government extend to such acts only as are injurious to others*. But it does me no injury for my neighbour to say there are twenty gods, or no god. It neither picks my pocket nor breaks my leg."[30] [emphasis added]

Jefferson echoes Locke, as Samuel Adams did in 1772, that not only is it impossible for inalienable rights to be forcibly taken away, but that it is impossible for them even to be voluntarily given away. They may be violated, but they cannot cease to adhere to the individual.

Jefferson is actually even more libertarian than Locke on atheism. Locke had argued for toleration of all religious beliefs except atheism, on the grounds that atheism would invalidate all oaths in court. Jefferson dismisses this objection:

"If it be said, his testimony in a court of justice cannot be relied on, reject it then, and be the stigma on him. Constraint may make him worse by making him a hypocrite, but it will never make him a truer man."[31]

When the time came for libertarians and conservatives to have it out, the previously Burkean conservatives split. Some, like John Adams, formed an uneasy alliance with the centralists to form the Federalist Party, seeing Jeffersonian libertarianism as a greater threat than centralization. Others threw in with the libertarians. Although they did not fight a war on the battlefield, the ideological armies were very much like that of the Revolutionary War. Hobbesian centralist conservatives on one side and a coalition between libertarians and Burkean constitutional conservatives on the other.

Libertarians hold the line

The Constitution represented an attempt by Hobbesian conservatives to reestablish the old order, with power centralized in a national government that was empowered to pass "all laws whatsoever." The conservatives were for the most part defeated, not only in the Constitution's limits on power to those enumerated, but in the resoundingly libertarian Bill of Rights. Because the first two proposed amendments were not adopted, the First Amendment provides an even more poetically libertarian opening, "Congress shall make no law..."

The libertarian victory was far from absolute. The Constitution did create a much more powerful government that *did* mirror Great Britain's more closely. While generally supportive of it, Jefferson's objections revolved around suspicion of the executive branch, which he considered too similar to monarchy, particularly with its lack of term limits. The power to tax the people directly was also a monumental increase in power, as was the power to regulate commerce.

But the real shift towards conservatism occurred in the first elections after ratification. More organized than their opposition and buoyed by universal admiration for Washington, the Federalists dominated the first six elections, resulting in Hamilton serving as the first Treasury Secretary for the better part of Washington's tenure in office. Hamilton would set the political and economic agenda for his party and conservatism in general, especially in his many reports to Congress, including his First Report on Public Credit, Operations of the Act Laying Duties on Imports, Second Report on Public Credit and Report on Manufactures.

In these documents lay the mercantilist economic agenda that to a large extent still dominates conservative economic policy today. Its chief tenets were a high protectionist tariff to assist domestic manufacturers, government subsidization of "infrastructure," which at that time meant roads and canals, and a central bank. These remained conservative domestic policies during the Federalist, Whig and Republican Party eras.

During the Adams administration, Hamilton made also political inroads in realizing a large standing army, at least in "quasi-peacetime" as the young nation found itself in the so-called Quasi War with France. Based upon his Hobbesian view of the relationship between nations, Hamilton yearned to expand the "American empire," first by dispossessing Spain of its colonial possession in the Americas. His constant wish for "national greatness" is the foundation of modern conservative claims of "American exceptionalism" in the "New American Century."

Economist Thomas Dilorenzo calls Hamilton's pervasive influence "Hamilton's Curse" in his book so titled. Lamenting the eventual triumph of Hamilton's ideas, he writes,

"The political legacy of Alexander Hamilton reads like a catalog of the ills of modern government: an out-of-control, unaccountable, monopolistic bureaucracy in Washington, D.C.; the demise of the Constitution as a restraint on the federal government's powers; the end of the idea that the citizens of the states should be the masters, rather than the servants, of their government; generations of activist federal judges who have eviscerated the constitutional protections of individual liberty in America; national debt; harmful protectionist international trade policies; corporate welfare (that is, the use of tax dollars to subsidize various politically connected businesses); and central economic planning and political control of the money supply, which have instigated boom-and-bust cycles in the economy."[32]

At the time, however, most of Hamilton's ideas were defeated or only minimally implemented. His one great victory was establishment of the First Bank of the United States. His Act Laying Duties on Imports was defeated in Congress and his army quickly disbanded when peace was achieved in the waning days of the Adams administration.

Nevertheless, Hamilton's vision of a strong central government, mercantilist economic policy and large, active military establishment formed the basis for conservatism in America thereafter.

The Revolution of 1800

It was these ideas which Thomas Jefferson sought to defeat in the elections of 1796 and 1800, the latter resulting in his inauguration as president and a Republican majority in Congress. Jefferson viewed the differences between the parties as so significant that he later called the election a second revolution. Applauding Judge Spencer Roane's published letters condemning the Supreme Court decision McCullough vs. Maryland, Jefferson wrote to their author:

"They contain the true principles of the revolution of 1800, for that was as real a revolution in the principles of our government as that of 1776 was in its form;"[33]

The principles Jefferson refers to are the libertarian principles which he and the Republicans believed should guide and limit the federal government's power. There is no mystery concerning what they were. Jefferson articulated them clearly in his first inaugural address:

"Let us, then, with courage and confidence pursue our own Federal and Republican principles, our attachment to union and representative government. Kindly separated by nature and a wide ocean from the exterminating havoc of one quarter of the globe; too high-minded to endure the degradations of the others; possessing a chosen country, with room enough for our descendants to the thousandth and thousandth generation; entertaining a due sense of our equal right to the use of our own faculties, to the acquisitions of our own industry, to honor and confidence from our fellow-citizens, resulting not from birth, but from our actions and their sense of them; enlightened by a benign religion, professed, indeed, and practiced in various forms, yet all of them inculcating honesty, truth, temperance, gratitude, and the love of man;

acknowledging and adoring an overruling Providence, which by all its dispensations proves that it delights in the happiness of man here and his greater happiness hereafter -- with all these blessings, what more is necessary to make us a happy and a prosperous people? Still one thing more, fellow-citizens -- a wise and frugal Government, *which shall restrain men from injuring one another, shall leave them otherwise free to regulate their own pursuits of industry and improvement,* and shall not take from the mouth of labor the bread it has earned. This is the sum of good government, and this is necessary to close the circle of our felicities."[34] [emphasis added]

Remember this passage. This is the President of the United States proclaiming in his inaugural address the enforcement of the libertarian non-aggression principle as the purpose of government. Again demonstrating his gift for succinctness, he incorporates Locke's resulting theory of property rights and makes a case for a free market all in one sentence.

All government action is inherently violent. The government response to even the smallest violation of its laws is a violent one. If you ignore a parking ticket, you will get some nasty letters before anyone actually knocks at your door. But if you ignore the nasty letters, eventually men with guns will come to get you. That is the nature of government. It is nothing more than the organized brute force of the whole community.

All three philosophies we've studied recognize this. They disagree on when it is appropriate to use that violent force. Jefferson here articulates the libertarian view that it can only be used in response to aggression by one person or group against another.

Jefferson would reiterate his libertarian stance again in his second inaugural, while rejecting Rousseau at the same time:

"…that the public efforts may be directed honestly to the public good, that peace be cultivated, civil and religious liberty unassailed, law and order preserved; equality of rights maintained, *and that state of property, equal or unequal, which results to every man from his own industry, or that of his fathers*."[35] [emphasis added]

This fundamental difference between Jefferson's Republicans and the French Jacobins not only eluded Jefferson's critics, it apparently eluded Jefferson and his Republicans as well. They were enthusiastic supporters of the French Revolution, despite its horrors correctly attributed by conservatives to unrestrained democracy and the resulting violations of property rights.

Jefferson similarly admired Thomas Paine's **Rights of Man**, despite its very unlibertarian proposal to construct an early version of the modern welfare state. This was completely inconsistent not only with Jefferson's statements in the two inaugurals, but with his warning to "prevent the government from wasting the labors of the people under the pretense of taking care of them."[36] Jefferson was apparently able to ignore the parts he didn't like, just as he did with the French Revolution.

While certainly antithetical to Rousseau's, Jefferson's agenda was actually directed at Hamilton's conservative economic system with its government-directed and subsidized economy. His first inaugural once again affirms his belief that the purpose of government is to enforce the non-aggression principle and otherwise leave individuals free, which is impossible if their government overrides their ability to "dispose of their persons and possessions as they see fit" and instead expropriates them to subsidize government projects. On this point, libertarians part with conservatives of all stripes.

The Lockean libertarian ideas Jefferson articulated in his inaugurals were not just nice words to be pondered and discussed in salons. They for the most part informed his policies in the real world.

Jefferson made good on his promises to eliminate the internal taxes levied by the Federalists. The cuts were funded by deep cuts in the military. As the army had already been disbanded by Congress during the Adams administration, Jefferson sought to reduce the navy to one consistent with the libertarian principle that the military, like the government as a whole, should be limited to a defensive force. Besides those ships absolutely necessary to protect American commercial shipping, Jefferson wanted the navy reduced to "gun boats for the defence of harbors, and of other smooth and enclosed waters."[37]

"It must be superfluous to observe, that this species of naval armament is proposed merely for defensive operation; that it can have but little effect toward protecting our commerce in the open seas even on our coast; and still less can it become an excitement to engage in offensive maritime war, toward which it would furnish no means."[38]

Jefferson was by no means perfectly consistent in limiting his actions as president either by the principle of non-aggression or by his own professed strict construction of the constitution. Biographer R. B. Bernstein actually lauds his departure from both:

"Despite his general commitment to a narrow interpretation of the Constitution, Jefferson wielded executive power with vigor and skill; his first term's greatest achievements showed his willingness to test the constitutional limits of presidential power. In sending a naval expedition to punish the Barbary Pirates, or acquiring from France the port of New Orleans and the territory of Louisiana, or planning the Lewis and Clark Expedition to explore those western territories, Jefferson showed himself to be a versatile, adaptable chief executive."[39]

Bernstein also notes Jefferson's inconsistency in his personal life. While philosophically opposed to slavery, he chose at the time of his father-in-law's death to assume ownership of lands and slaves instead of liquidating them and paying off debts attached to them. The decision made Jefferson one of the largest slaveholders in Virginia.

It also saddled him with debt he would never be able to repay. Liquidating the lands and slaves would have made him financially more secure and morally more consistent. Contrary to 21st century arguments that libertarianism is "utopian," the libertarian approach would have been infinitely more practical for Jefferson, even within a "slave economy."

The most "unlibertarian" aspect of Jefferson's public policy, however, was his support for public education. In fairness, Jefferson did not see education of those who cannot afford it as a right that the government could force others to underwrite, but rather a protection against the danger their ignorance posed in a democratic republic. His view at least hints at a touch of conservatism, fearing that uneducated, "unwashed masses" will run roughshod over the rights and property of individuals if not educated properly to act otherwise.

Ironically, he sees education as both Hobbes and Rousseau do, not merely or even primarily to teach reading, writing and arithmetic, but to instill proper political principles, only in his case, libertarian. They are first on his list of objectives of higher education:

"To form the statesmen, legislators and judges, on whom public prosperity and individual happiness are so much to depend; To expound the principles and structure of government, the laws, which regulate the intercourse of nations, those formed municipally for our own government, and a sound spirit of legislation, which, banishing all arbitrary and unnecessary restraint on individual action, *shall leave us free to do whatever does not violate the equal rights of one another.*"[40] [emphasis added]

Jefferson would be horrified to learn of the "progressive" liberal philosophy taught instead in 21st century American public schools. Modern libertarians are correct to criticize him for supporting tax subsidized institutions, even to teach principles they agree with. Using Jefferson's own reasoning on most other matters, the power itself is only an election away from being used otherwise.

Despite these inconsistencies and the political fallout from his ill-advised embargo, Jefferson and the Republicans did succeed in reversing the conservative trend in federal politics, establishing principles that would endure for decades. These included low tariffs, adequate for revenue but not significantly protecting domestic manufacturers from foreign competition, prohibitions on the federal government for most "infrastructure" building, and a small, defensive military establishment during peacetime.

American foreign policy would be consistently noninterventionist for an entire century, regardless of which party was in power. There were two declared wars during that time, but both were fought in response to acts of war committed by the enemy nation, at least in pretense. President after president reiterated Washington and Jefferson's policy to stay out of overseas conflicts in their inaugural addresses.

Jefferson was unable to get rid of the national bank. While Madison let the bank lapse only reluctantly, despite his earlier arguments as to its unconstitutionality, he eventually called for and signed into law the Second Bank of the United States. It would die a similar death to the first at the end of its twenty year charter. What followed was a period known as "free banking" that did not completely end until creation of the Federal Reserve System in 1913.

The Whigs and the American System

So complete was the defeat of the Federalists and the rejection of their ideas that the party eventually dissolved. However, the conservative movement did not die with it and eventually a new party emerged, reviving the old Hamiltonian platform as their own.

Led by Henry Clay of Kentucky, the Whigs fought for the better part of three decades to install Clay's "American System," which was substantially Hamilton's domestic policy of protective tariffs, government-subsidized "internal improvements (infrastructure)" and a national bank. For the most part, they had the same success as the Federalists after 1800: none.

Nevertheless, the Whigs were critically important in the history of American politics. Despite their failure to remake the United States into a new British Empire, as Hamilton had wanted, they kept the conservative movement alive and organized while Jeffersonian republicanism and later Jacksonian democracy were ascendant. They were to reform once again under a new party, this time with vastly different results.

Lincoln and the Republicans

After the dissolution of the Whig's in the 1850's, another party emerged to take up the Hamiltonian cause. Jefferson's Democratic-Republicans had split in 1824 between "Democrats" supporting Andrew Jackson and the short-lived "National Republicans" supporting John Quincy Adams. Since Jefferson's party was now simply called the Democratic Party, conservatives ironically adopted the name formerly used by their arch rivals: Republican.

All things being equal, the prospects for the new Republican Party were no better than they had been for the Whigs or Federalists. Support for Clay's American System remained low. But all things were not equal, pun intended.

The slavery issue, simmering for decades, had finally come to a boil. The abolitionist movement represented a significant constituency with which conservatives could ally to finally realize electoral success. That is not to say that most conservatives did not oppose slavery or that the alliance was purely a cynical one on the part of conservatives to exploit opposition to slavery for their own ends. Hamilton himself had been a fierce opponent of the institution and made many unsuccessful attempts to weaken or abolish it. But it was this alliance that finally allowed conservatives to install the American System after more than sixty years of failure.

Georgia recognized the alliance in its Declaration of the Causes of Secession:

"The party of Lincoln, called the Republican party, under its present name and organization, is of recent origin. It is admitted to be an anti-slavery party. *While it attracts to itself by its creed the scattered advocates of exploded political heresies, of condemned theories in political economy, the advocates of commercial restrictions, of protection, of special privileges, of waste and corruption in the administration of Government,* anti-slavery is its mission and its purpose. By anti-slavery it is made a power in the state."[41]

Ironically, slavery wasn't even Lincoln's primary motivation, neither in seeking the presidency nor in prosecuting the Civil War. On the former subject, Lincoln was as unambiguous during his campaign as he would be in his first inaugural.

"Through all, I have neither assailed, nor wrestled with any part of the constitution. The legal right of the Southern people to reclaim their fugitives I have constantly admitted. The legal right of Congress to interfere with their institution in the states, I have constantly denied. In resisting the spread of slavery to new territory, and with that, what appears to me to be a tendency to subvert the first principle of free government itself my whole effort has consisted. To the best of my judgment, I have labored for and not against the Union."[42]

On the latter, Lincoln was equally clear, even as late as 1862:

"My paramount object in this struggle is to save the Union, and is not either to save or destroy slavery. If I could save the Union without freeing any slave I would do it, and if I could save it by freeing all the slaves I would do it; and if I could save it by freeing some and leaving others alone I would also do that. What I do about slavery, and the colored race, I do because I believe it helps to save the Union; and I forbear because I do not believe it would help to save the Union."[43]

Slavery is completely antithetical to Locke's philosophy and libertarianism. Locke barely took the time to deal with it in his Second Treatise, concluding in just a few paragraphs that slavery "is nothing else, but the state of war continued."[44] Yet, it was primarily the southern, slaveholding states who seemed to advance libertarian principles in the pre-Civil War era and northern, non-slaveholding states who opposed them.

This is to a large extent due to the comparative advantages that geography gave the two regions, respectively. The south had a longer growing season and more fertile soil, both of which better supported large plantations, which were more adaptable to slave labor. Thus, even southerners like Jefferson who opposed the institution philosophically had a financial incentive to continue it.

More importantly, even the libertarian-minded southerners who opposed government power in most other areas often thought like conservatives on the subject of slavery. They feared what might happen if the slaves were freed too suddenly, without allowing for their education and the establishment in them of regard for the principles of civilized society. Some, including Jefferson, also feared they would seek revenge on their former masters, once freed and presumably afforded their rights to bear arms.

This resulted in a novel idea supported by both Jefferson and, later, Lincoln. As nobody on any side believed the former slaves could live peacefully with the rest of American society, members of both major parties attempted to adopt the policy of freeing the slaves and then extricating them from the continent. Calling the program "colonization," the intent was to send some of the former slaves back to Africa, some to the West Indies and others to new colonies in South America. Regardless of their positions on the institution of slavery, almost no one believed black people were "created equal," least of all Lincoln:

"I will say then that I am not, nor ever have been, in favor of bringing about in any way the social and political equality of the white and black races, [applause]-that I am not nor ever have been in favor of making voters or jurors of negroes, nor of qualifying them to hold office, nor to intermarry with white people; and I will say in addition to this that there is a physical difference between the white and black races which I believe will forever forbid the two races living together on terms of social and political equality."[45]

Lincoln was as much a "man of his times" as Jefferson had been and as were most opponents of slavery in his own time. There is no reason to doubt Lincoln's sincerity on his personal opposition to slavery. Yet, statements like this and many others leave little room for doubt that Lincoln, like most of his contemporaries, viewed black people as inferior.

The Confederacy's argument was a Burkean constitutional one. The reason put forth for secession by the southern states was the federal government was not delegated the power to make laws regarding slavery within the states, either to abolish it, curtail it or even promote it.

It's the same concept as in the Star Trek episode. The Federation didn't approve of the Vulcan practice of requiring mortal combat to settle courtship disputes, but they weren't delegated any power to regulate that aspect of Vulcan life. They were only delegated power to defend the Federation planets against the Klingons and Romulans.

The idea that slavery could not be ended abruptly, freeing millions of people who were unprepared for freedom, was also firmly rooted in Burkean conservative thinking. Mississippi's Declaration contains this sentiment:

"It seeks not to elevate or to support the slave, but to destroy his present condition without providing a better."[46]

It is also important to remember the order of events. All of the southern states did not secede at the same time. Seven of the slave states seceded before Lincoln took office. Virginia, Arkansas, Tennessee and North Carolina did not secede until Lincoln called for troops to invade the southern states.

They intentionally waited to see if Lincoln would violate the American Creed's "right to alter or abolish" they believed the seceding states were exercising, just as the colonies had in 1776. Lincoln reacted just as King George III had towards the colonies.

That's not to say the Confederate states were completely in the right. Whenever a war kills hundreds of thousands of people, there is plenty of blame to go around on both sides. Some southerners just plain supported slavery. Those who didn't sure picked a rotten issue over which to dig in.

The principle of limited powers delegated to the federal government was an important one. That the southern states made their stand for this principle over slavery was a tragedy for future generations of Americans.

To this day, *any* resistance to centralization of federal power is conflated with slavery or racism, both by proponents of centralization and honest people just trying to figure out what's right. Southern politicians using "states' rights" and nullification arguments to oppose desegregation of schools during the civil rights era further reinforced this misconception.

It all goes back to the futility of looking for good guys and bad guys when studying history. Both north and south was a mixture of people partially standing up for principles they believed in and partially choosing their own self-interest over the right thing to do. They were human beings, capable of good and evil, just as Locke saw them.

Rather than trying to make one side more right than another, the most elegant explanation for what caused the tragic war is to simply take everyone at their word. The southern states opposed northern mercantilism, but tolerated it. It was their perception that slavery would eventually be abolished that pushed them far enough to secede.

Similarly, the northern states opposed slavery, but were willing to allow it to continue where it already existed. What they weren't willing to tolerate was the secession of the southern states, for any reason. That begs the question, "Why not?"

Lincoln's Hobbesian conservatism

If not the abolition of slavery, what was Lincoln's "real agenda?" Dilorenzo provides one answer:

"Lincoln was always a Whig and was almost single-mindedly devoted to the Whig agenda – protectionism, government control of the money supply through a nationalized banking system, and government subsidies for railroad, shipping, and canal-building businesses ("internal improvements").[47]

Lincoln's own words confirm this. In his very first political speech in 1832, he quipped,

"I presume you all know who I am. I am humble Abraham Lincoln. I have been solicited by many friends to become a candidate for the Legislature. My politics are short and sweet, like the old woman's dance. I am in favor of a national bank. I am in favor of the internal improvement system, and a high protective tariff. These are my sentiments and political principles. If elected, I shall be thankful; if not it will be all the same."[48]

While Lincoln's devotion to Whig leader Henry Clay's "American System" cannot be denied, it does not tell the whole story of his worldview. As for Burke, the mercantilist system for Lincoln was merely the economic expression of the larger conservative philosophy. Lincoln is certainly more Hobbesian, but as early as his first inaugural we hear him make what by now is a familiar conservative argument, common to Hobbes and Burke:

"I hold that in contemplation of universal law and of the Constitution the Union of these States is perpetual. Perpetuity is implied, if not expressed, in the fundamental law of all national governments. It is safe to assert that no government proper ever had a provision in its organic law for its own termination. Continue to execute all the express provisions of our National Constitution, and the Union will endure forever, it being impossible to destroy it except by some action not provided for in the instrument itself."[49]

As Burke argued in *Reflections* and Hobbes did in *Leviathan*, Lincoln maintains that once the government is constituted, it is perpetual and cannot be dissolved, regardless of the grievances of any of its constituents. The commonwealth, or "the Union," in Lincoln's parlance, must be preserved at all costs. It is the only means of resisting a return to the awful state of nature between individuals and civil war between local polities.

His statement that "no government proper ever had a provision in its organic law for its own termination" flatly contradicts the organic law articulated in the American Creed, that the people have a natural, inalienable right to alter or abolish the government if it fails to secure their rights.

You may agree with Lincoln or the Creed, but you can't agree with both.

Lincoln goes on to raise the familiar conservative specter of anarchy as the only alternative to an indivisible Union:

"Plainly the central idea of secession is the essence of anarchy. A majority held in restraint by constitutional checks and limitations, and always changing easily with deliberate changes of popular opinions and sentiments, is the only true sovereign of a free people. Whoever rejects it does of necessity fly to anarchy or to despotism. Unanimity is impossible. The rule of a minority, as a permanent arrangement, is wholly inadmissible; so that, rejecting the majority principle, anarchy or despotism in some form is all that is left."[50]

Rank and file troops shared Lincoln's conservative fear of anarchy, as James M. McPherson observes:

"This contest is not the North against the South," wrote a young Philadelphia printer six days before he enlisted. 'It is government against anarchy, law against disorder.' An Indiana lawyer who rose to brigadier general during the war and secretary of state after it told his pacifist wife in April 1861 that 'it is better to have war for one year than anarchy & revolution for fifty years – If the government should suffer rebels to go on with their work with impunity there would be no end to it & in a short time we would be without any law or order."[51]

Lincoln and mercantilism

These conservative political arguments may have been merely convenient for Lincoln, who was more concerned with his conservative economic program. The secession of the southern states presented him with two problems, one geometrically increasing the effect of the other.

First, he was losing a substantial portion of the tax base his internal improvement program relied on. The south claimed it was paying the majority of federal taxes due to it being a largely agrarian region, relying more heavily than the north on imports for manufactured items. That claim is disputed, but whether the southern states paid a majority or a substantial minority of federal taxes, it was revenue Lincoln could ill afford to lose.

Second, the anti-protectionist southern states would constitute a "free trade zone" on the Union's border. This threatened to take a huge portion of federal tax revenue away from the states remaining in the Union, due to the opportunity lower tariffs in the southern states offered to foreign exporters.

There is no way Lincoln could have continued even those few subsidies already in place with these substantially smaller tax revenues, much less pursue the massive expansions in government spending he intended.

The indivisibility of the sovereign power

Regardless, Lincoln's appeal to the indivisibility of the Union appealed to his conservative base, as did his many religious references. While Lincoln himself was not a churchgoer, the perennial conservative maxim that the central government was ordained by God was a central theme during the Civil War. Conservatives believed literally that they were fighting a holy war to preserve God's will, reflected in the Union's unofficial anthem, Battle Hymn of the Republic. As Henry W. Bellows famously opined,

"The head of a nation *is* a sacred person, representing, for the time he holds office, the most valuable and solemn rights and duties of a people. "The Government" is "upon his shoulder" – and the Government is the mighty pillar that fastens in order and holds to safety the ten thousand varying interests, rights and obligations of a nation. File at the staple which God fastens to his own throne, in the oaths of office which make a man chief ruler of a people, and you loosen thoughtlessly every link in that chain of law and order, which binds society together."[52]

Not only does Bellows reiterate the conservative plank that established government is ordained by God to save people from their own barbarous natures; he also expresses a distinctly Hobbesian strain of conservatism, investing divine authority in the chief executive. This represented a direct affront to both libertarianism and the more Burkean conservatism of the South, both of which would have abhorred Bellows' arguments for different reasons.

George M. Frederickson sees the Civil War as releasing "ultraconservatism" from its previous repression in the American consciousness.

"If Lieber and Thompson had been careful to make it clear that absolute obedience to the state was appropriate only where free institutions had been established, there were other publicists who went further and affirmed, or came dangerously close to affirming, the heretical doctrine that *all* well-established governments are ordained by God and deserve the unconditional fealty of their subjects. This willingness to use the war situation to affirm a pre-Lockean view of the social order, a conservative doctrine that went beyond the needs of the hour, suggest the latent vitality of an ultraconservatism which had been under wraps before the war, but now, for the moment at least, was coming into the open and flourishing in an emotion-charged atmosphere which was discrediting the very thought of rebellion or revolution."[53]

The Hobbesian victory

Indeed, the election of Lincoln and his Republicans in Congress was a conservative revolution, finally realizing the victory that had eluded the Federalists and Whigs for sixty years. In order to achieve it, conservatives had to ally themselves with a constituency advocating radical change, the abolition of slavery. This wasn't as difficult as one might think, for two reasons.

First, conservatives in the north had always opposed slavery and taken the lead on the few attempts to abolish or weaken it. Alexander Hamilton was a fierce critic of the institution, as was Lincoln. Too often, critics of Hamilton's or Lincoln's other political positions attempt to cast doubt on the sincerity of their opposition to slavery. There is no reason to do so. There is nothing inherently inconsistent with opposition to slavery and support of a centralized, mercantilist state.

Second, the Republican victory was a completely regional one. Support for all of Lincoln's policies, including prohibition of slavery in new territories, was concentrated in the industrial north, where slavery was already largely abolished by the states. For most Republicans, abolishing slavery was something that would happen somewhere else. They did not face the prospect of radical change within their own communities. It would occur in what was for all intents and purposes a completely different country, one which also opposed the mercantilist polices that Republicans sincerely believed in.

Southern conservatives, on the other hand, had completely the opposite view. Those who opposed slavery in principle took the conservative stance that any change must be gradual or made when the individual state was ready for it. Many, such as Robert E. Lee, freed their own slaves voluntarily, but took the political position that the state ultimately retained the power to decide the question constitutionally, regardless of their personal opposition to the institution.

Other southerners defended the institution outright, including from a religious perspective, based upon the Old Testament's support of the institution within the context of its narrative. Not only could they defend the institution itself on these grounds, but the Constitution's support of the institution. Consistent with conservative thinking, the Constitution as the sovereign power and, by then, the long-established tradition, could be assumed to be the will of God. As Eugene Genovese observes,

"Southerners rejected the argument at its root, insisting that slavery conformed to the Word of God and that, therefore, so did the Constitution of the United States, which, while itself not God's Word, was designed to be consistent to it."[54]

The idea that some people were simply born to be slaves fits into the conservative worldview, within which a hierarchy in society is both necessary and natural. Certainly, not all conservatives take the idea this far, as most in the English and American conservative traditions were the institution's fiercest critics. But it does have ancient roots in conservatism that predate Christianity. Aristotle, arguably "the original conservative," takes great pains to establish it, finally concluding:

"It is clear, then, that some men are by nature free, and others slaves, and that for these latter slavery is both expedient and right."[55]

In many ways, the American Civil War mirrored the American Revolution. A powerful national government, dominated by the more Hobbesian, centralizing brand of conservatism responded to a rebellion by a coalition of more Burkean, federalist conservatives and libertarians. The basis of the conflict was constitutional; it was fought to determine whether the southern states were free to secede or not. That was Lincoln's stated reason for the war, despite ubiquitous attempts to connect it with slavery, over his frequent objections.

But slavery, free trade, tariffs, corporate subsidies for internal improvements and other areas of dispute were all in the air, slavery being the most pressing issue at the moment.

Like the British, the Union attempted to exploit slavery both for popular support and for tactical advantage. Stripped of local prejudice, there is nothing substantively different between Lincoln's Emancipation Proclamation and General Johnny Burgoyne's offer to free any slave who fought with the British against the colonists. Both were simply war tactics, designed to cause chaos behind enemy lines through servile insurrection. Had Lincoln's been anything more, it would have freed slaves everywhere in the United States, rather than only in counties under Confederate control in seceded states.

Slavery was certainly abolished more quickly in the southern states than it would have been if the war had never been fought. The Thirteenth Amendment passed specifically because the states who would have opposed it were forced to ratify it as a condition of regaining their constitutional standing.

At the same time, it is unreasonable to argue that slavery would *never* have been abolished if the southern states had been allowed to peacefully secede. Every other civilized nation in the world abolished slavery without a destructive civil war, some long after the United States. Apologists for the southern states argue that slavery was already dying before the war. Apologists for the Union dispute this. Almost nobody believes there would be slaves in the 21st century had the war not been fought.

What is almost universally overlooked are the rest of the consequences of the war for the future of the United States. Along with abolishing slavery, the war crushed virtually all elements of both libertarianism and Burkean conservatism in American politics. The political and economic agenda of the Federalists and Whigs was finally established after six decades of failure. In many ways, America would never be the same.

At the constitutional level, all pretense that the Union is a voluntary compact between otherwise sovereign states was eliminated. New York, Virginia and Rhode Island had only ratified the Constitution on the condition that they could secede if the federal government didn't obey it. The southern states had seceded for specifically that reason. They were, Virginia included, treated as rebels and answered with force.

The internal improvements program was established, never to be challenged again. Subsidization of the railroads, government roads and other "infrastructure" became universally recognized as government functions, with all of the attending inefficiency, fraud and waste. By 1915, Seymour Dunbar had traced the slow death of America's spectacular private road system to the Civil War:

"Many of the toll road franchises have only lapsed in recent years, and a few are still effective. Maryland, and perhaps other states, yet possess toll-gates. Not until after the Civil War did the various commonwealths generally adopt a policy under which roadways were considered public works to be created and maintained by the people themselves and used without toll fees."[56]

Lincoln and the Republicans did not create a Third Bank of the United States, but they did reintroduce fiat currency and nationalized banking with the National Banking Acts of 1863 and 1864.

High protectionist tariffs became the norm for the rest of the century, with few exceptions. The idea that consumers should pay higher prices and thus suffer a lower standard of living in order to protect domestic manufacturers became entrenched in American thinking. It's now considered patriotic to "buy American." At one time, this idea was fiercely resisted by Jeffersonians in the north and south.

Government control of the economy became increasingly centralized during the period of Republican domination after the war, beginning with Lincoln's creation of a U.S. Department of Agriculture (1862) and continuing with Teddy Roosevelt's Department of Commerce and Labor (1903). The latter eventually became two federal departments and a federal regulatory agency: the Department of Commerce, Department of Labor and Federal Trade Commission, respectively.

Republicans also passed the Sherman Anti-Trust Act. This was a fundamental attack on private property ownership, specifically the inherent right to "dispose of one's possessions as one sees fit" as Locke would say. This legislation and subsequent bills like it make buying and selling private property a privilege, rather than a right, requiring permission by the sovereign. It's standard, anti-free market conservatism, right out of Hobbes or Burke.

Although sold to the public as protection against "trusts" like Standard Oil, the law was actually just more protectionism of connected corporations. Standard Oil and companies like it dominated the market at the time because they were more efficient and offered consumers lower prices. Today, liberals and conservatives both promote a fantastic theory that these trusts were only lowering their prices until they eliminated all competitors. Then, at some magic moment, they were going to raise prices dramatically. Dilorenzo responds directly to this hoary canard:

"True, one might say, the trusts were dropping prices. But weren't they just doing this temporarily in hopes of driving all the competition from the market? This, of course, would have been the height of economic folly – to drop your price below cost *for several decades* in hope of someday making a monopoly profit. And remember, even John D. Rockefeller's Standard Oil faced hundreds of competitors, so it would have been rather difficult to drive out all competition."[57] [emphasis in the original]

New federal departments, higher regulation, centralized regulation of banking, corporate subsidies for infrastructure and high protectionist tariffs all became policy during the post-Civil War period. The moved significantly away from laissez faire free markets and towards a more conservative mercantilist system.

In short, the Civil War and the dominance of the Republican Party in the decades that followed allowed the Hobbesian centralizers to win an absolute victory and largely recreate the socio-economic system of Great Britain, after decades of failure before the war. It didn't just overturn sixty years of elections. In many ways, it overturned the Revolutionary War itself. Americans were now subject to an economic system a lot like the one they had seceded from Great Britain to escape.

One might argue that the imperial aspect of classical Hobbesian conservatism was missing, but that's not entirely true, either. Before expanding beyond the borders of the United States, the centralizers had to subdue the states themselves. The Civil War accomplished that.

The next threat came from Native American nations existing within the borders of the United States. That challenge to the sovereign power took several decades after the Civil War to dispose of.

When Native Americans no longer posed a significant threat, American imperialism began, virtually on cue. In 1898, the Hobbesians finally got their war with Spain, resulting in acquisition of several Spanish colonial possessions. Alexander Hamilton smiled in his grave.

It was the first step in building a new kind of empire; one which did not annex new territory but exercised a political and economic dominance over the entire world, backed by unchallenged military might. This would take all of the 20th century to realize, advanced by conservatives and liberals alike, for different reasons based upon their philosophical differences.

The United States headed into their second full century substantially transformed from what they had been at the outset of their first. The federal government was far more conservative and the economy far more mercantilist than it had been before the dominance of the Republican Party.

But all aspects of libertarianism were not eliminated. Burkean conservatism was helpful in this respect. Regardless of their inherent contradiction with core conservative principles, Jefferson's ideas had become long-established legal tradition by the time conservatives finally came into power. Just as they now defend the New Deal and may someday defend Obamacare, conservatives defended libertarianism even as they vanquished it.

Within the framework of conservative interventions, a market economy still functioned. Despite the many departures in practice, the stated purpose of government was still Jefferson's libertarian one throughout the 19th century.

As the 20th century dawned, that was about to change.

End of Part One

Next: Chapter Six The Creed in Exile:
The Liberals Strike Back

About the Author

Tom Mullen is the author of *A Return to Common Sense: Reawakening Liberty in the Inhabitants of America*. His work has appeared in The Washington Times, The Huffington Post, Rare and numerous other publications. Tom holds a B.A. in English from Canisius College and an M.A. in English from Buffalo State College. Tom is also a singer/songwriter with several CD releases, both as a solo musician and with his band, The Skeptics. He resides with his family in Western New York.

Notes

Chapter One Something is Wrong with the World

[1] *The Matrix* (1999) Warner Bros. Pictures

[2] Stars and Stripes July 8, 2014 http://www.stripes.com/news/middle-east/1-000-syrian-rebels-defect-to-islamic-state-activists-say-1.292493

[3] Paltrow, Scott J. "Unaccountable: The high cost of the Pentagon's bad bookkeeping" Reuters November 18, 2013 http://www.reuters.com/investigates/pentagon/#article/part2

[4] Tenth Amendment Center http://tenthamendmentcenter.com/2014/02/12/utah-legislator-introduces-bill-to-cut-of-nsa-data-centers-water-supply/

[5] The Guardian January 25, 2014 http://www.theguardian.com/commentisfree/2014/jan/25/obama-administration-military-torture-army-field-manual

[6] Werner, Erica Huffington Post http://www.huffingtonpost.com/2011/03/31/obama-accepts-transparenc_n_843195.html

[7] http://www.gallup.com/poll/170750/despite-enrollment-success-healthcare-law-remains-unpopular.aspx

[8] Rasmussen Report http://www.rasmussenreports.com/public_content/politics/obama_administration/daily_presidential_tracking_poll

9 "CORPORATE CONDUCT: THE PRESIDENT; Bush Signs Bill Aimed at Fraud In Corporations" by Elizabeth Bumiller New York Times July 31, 2002 http://www.nytimes.com/2002/07/31/business/corporate-conduct-the-president-bush-signs-bill-aimed-at-fraud-in-corporations.html.

[10] http://www.taxpolicycenter.org/taxfacts/displayafact.cfm?Docid=200 Note: The U.S. government fiscal year runs October 1 – Sept. 30, meaning that outgoing presidents actually propose the budget their successors will operate under during their first nine months in office.
[11] http://www.gpo.gov/fdsys/pkg/BUDGET-2008-BUD/pdf/BUDGET-2008-BUD-11.pdf

Chapter Two Where Do Conservatives Come From?

[1] Bolt, Robert A Man for All Seasons
[2] Hobbes, Thomas *Leviathan or The Matter, Forme and Power of a Common Wealth Ecclesiasticall and Civil* Hackett Publishing Company Indianapolis, IN 1994 pg. 76
[3] Hobbes Leviathan pg. 74
[4] Hobbes Leviathan pg. 75
[5] Hobbes Leviathan pg. 76
[6] Kirk, *Leviathan, I,* pg. 5
[7] Kirk, Russell *The Conservative Mind: From Burke to Eliot* Regnery Publishing; Seventh Edition (November 30, 1953) Kindle Edition Location 707 of 6718
[8] Hobbes Leviathan pg. 80
[9] Burke, Edmund *Reflections on the Revolution in France* Second Edition London Printed for J. Dodsley, in Pall-Mall 1790 pgs.88-89
[10] Kirk, *Conservative Mind,* Location 2144-2148
[11] Hobbes Leviathan pg. 106
[12] Kirk, *Conservative Mind,* Location 888 0f 6718
[13] Burke, *Reflections* pg. 33
[14] Hobbes Leviathan pg. 113
[15] Kirk, *Conservative Mind,* Location 661 of 6718
[16] Santorum, Rick from Rick Santorum 'It Takes a Family" interview on National Public Radio
http://www.npr.org/templates/story/story.php?storyId=4784905
[17] Boaz, David from Freedom Watch (Fox Business) January 4, 2012
https://www.youtube.com/watch?v=jTDAu6ENPVE
[18] Hobbes Leviathan pg. 114
[19] Kirk *Leviathan, I* pg. 5
[20] Kirk, *Conservative Mind,* Location 1111 of 6718
[21] Woods, Tom http://tomwoods.com/blog/someday-conservatives-will-defend-obamacare/
[22] Hobbes Leviathan pg. 121
[23] Massachusetts Constitution of 1780 http://www.nhinet.org/ccs/docs/ma-1780.htm
[24] Kirk, *Conservative Mind,* Location 739
[25] Kirk, *Conservative Mind,* Location 1062-1066
[26] Kirk, *Conservative Mind,* Location 1821

[27] Hobbes Leviathan pg. 140
[28] Hobbes Leviathan pg. 114
[29] Taft, Robert Speech on the North Atlantic Treaty July 26, 1949
http://teachingamericanhistory.org/library/document/speech-on-the-north-atlantic-treaty/

Chapter Three Where Do Liberals Come From?

[1] Roosevelt, Franklin Delano Speech before the 1936 Democratic National Convention Philadelphia, PA June 27, 1936
http://www.austincc.edu/lpatrick/his2341/fdr36acceptancespeech.htm
[2] Sirota, David "What's the Difference Between a Liberal and a Liberal" Huffington Post http://www.huffingtonpost.com/david-sirota/whats-the-difference-betw_b_9140.html
[3] Rousseau Discourse on the Origin of Inequality pg. 37
[4] Rousseau Discourse on the Origin of Inequality pg. 37
[5] Rousseau Discourse on the Origin of Inequality pg. 53
[6] Rousseau Discourse on the Origin of Inequality pg. 55
[7] Rousseau Discourse on the Origin of Inequality pg. 60
[8] Rousseau Discourse on the Origin of Inequality pg. 65
[9] Rousseau Discourse on the Origin of Inequality pg. 68
[10] Rousseau Discourse on the Origin of Inequality pg. 69
[11] Proudhon, Pierre Joseph . *What is Property? An Inquiry into the Principle of Right and of Government.* Electronic Text Center, University of Virginia Library
http://web.archive.org/web/20080830074011/http://etext.lib.virginia.edu/toc/modeng/public/ProProp.html
[12] Rousseau Discourse on Political Economy pg. 117
[13] Rousseau On the Social Contract pg. 148
[14] Rousseau On the Social Contract pg. 148
[15] Rousseau On the Social Contract pg. 156
[16] Rousseau On the Social Contract pg. 153
[17] Rousseau On the Social Contract pg. 154
[18] Rousseau Discourse on Political Economy pg. 124
[19] Rousseau Discourse on Political Economy pg. 125
[20] Rousseau On the Social Contract pg. 226
[21] Rousseau On the Social Contract pg. 173
[22] Rousseau On the Social Contract pg. 206
[23] Marx, Karl *The Communist Manifesto* Kindle Edition HarperTorch (February 11, 2014) Location 107
[24] Engels, Frederick *The Communist Manifesto* Location 303
[25] Marx *The Communist Manifesto* Location 113
[26] Marx *The Communist Manifesto* Location 615
[27] Marx *The Communist Manifesto* Location 333
[28] Marx The Communist Manifesto Location 432

[29] Marx *The Communist Manifesto* Location 451
[30] Marx *The Communist Manifesto* Location 451
[31] Madison, James Federalist #10 Library of Congress website
http://thomas.loc.gov/home/histdox/fed_10.html

Chapter Four Where Did the Founding Fathers Come From?

[1] Jefferson, Thomas Minutes of the Board of Visitors, University of Virginia March 4, 1825 from Jefferson Writings
[2] Gutzman, Kevin Ph.D. The Politically Incorrect Guide to the Constitution Regnery Publishing, Inc. Washington, D.C. 2007 pg. 31
[3] "Discourses on Government by Algernon Sydney, also cited in Jefferson's 1825 resolution, was a refutation of Sir Robert Filmer's *Patriarcha*, a defense of the divine right of kings. Locke undertook the same task in the first of his *Two Treatises of Government*. Locke and Sydney were both part of the Whig movement, with similar views on the nature of man, natural rights and purpose of government. As both Sydney's *Discourses* and Locke's *First Treatise* focus on refuting the divine right of kings, rather than specifically laying the foundation for a new theory of society and government, we will put them aside and concentrate on Locke's *Second Treatise*, in which he builds society and government up from the state of nature.
[4] Locke Second Treatise pgs. 72-3
[5] Locke Second Treatise pg. 73
[66] Locke Second Treatise pg. 73
[7] Locke Second Treatise pg. 80
[88] Locke Second Treatise pg. 80
[9] Locke Second Treatise pg. 81
[10] Locke Second Treatise pg. 76
[11] Locke Second Treatise pg. 109
[12] Locke Second Treatise pg. 109
[13] Locke Second Treatise pg. 110
[14] Locke Second Treatise pg. 112
[15] Locke Second Treatise pg. 112
[16] Locke begins by explaining that the name should be "parental power," because the mother has equal rights and responsibilities in the care and education of children.
[17] Locke Second Treatise pg. 100
[18] Locke Second Treatise pg. 113
[19] Locke Second Treatise pg. 111
[20] Locke Second Treatise pg. 138
[21] Locke Second Treatise pg. 138
[22] Declaration of Independence (1776)
[23] Smith, Adam *The Wealth of Nations* Kindle Edition location 12029 of 16850

[24] Tocqueville, Alexis de Democracy in America Kindle Edition location 12441 of 17633
[25] Locke Second Treatise pg. 125
[26] Twenty-Ninth Congress Sess. I Ch. 16
http://www.lawandfreedom.com/site/historical/Mexico1846.pdf

Chapter Five Defending the Creed: The Conservative Tide

[1] Adams, John A Dissertation on the Canon and the Feudal Law No. 1 from *Papers of John Adams* Harvard University Press 2003 pg. 112
[2] Smith, Adam from *How Adam Smith Can Change Your Life* by Russ Roberts Portfolio/Penguin New York, NY 2014 Kindle Edition Location 564 of 2682
[3] Bradford, William *Of Plymouth Plantation* edited by Caleb Johnson Xlibris 2006 Kindle Edition location 2405-2412
[4] Bradford Of Plymouth Plantation location 2418
[5] Bradford Of Plymouth Plantation location 2400-2405
[6] Dilorenzo, Thomas *How Capitalism Saved America* Three Rivers Press New York 2004 pg. 56
[7] Declaration of Rights and Grievances, (1765) from *Liberty Documents: With Contemporary Exposition and Critical Comments Drawn from Various Writers* Hill, Mabel Longmans, Green, and Co. 91 and 93 Fifth Avenue New York London and Bombay 1901 pg. 156
[8] Adams, Samuel *The Rights of the Colonists* (1772) The Report of the Committee of Correspondence to the Boston Town Meeting, Nov. 20, 1772 from Old South Leaflets no. 173 edited by Edwin Doak Mead Old South Meeting House 1903 pgs. 417-428.

[9] Locke Second Treatise
[10] Hobbes Leviathan pg.
[11] Sumner, William Graham *A History of American Currency* Henry Holt and Company 1874 Pg. 42
[12] Declaration of Independence (1776)
[13] Declaration of Independence (1776)
[14] Articles of Confederation (1778)
[15] Gutzman, Kevin, Ph.D., J.D. The Politically Incorrect Guide to the Constitution Regnery Publishing, Inc. Washington, D.C. 2007 pg. 176
[16] Hamilton, Alexander Letter to James Duane September 3, 1780 from *Hamilton Writings* Literary Classics of the United States, Inc., New York, NY 2001 pg. 70
[17] *Hamilton Writings*, pg. 73.
[18] Hamilton *Writings* pg. 44.
[19] Hamilton *Writings* pg. 156.
[20] Hamilton *Writings* pg. 166.

[21] Hamilton *Writings* pg. 149-50.

[22] Hamilton *Writings* pg. 165.

[23] Hamilton *Writings* pg. 149.

[24] Gutzman, Kevin Ph.D., J.D. *James Madison and the Making of America* St. Martin's Press, New York 2012 pg. 136

[25] Constitution of the Commonwealth of Massachusetts https://malegislature.gov/laws/constitution

[26] McCullough, David John Adams Simon & Schuster Paperbacks Rockefeller Center 1230 Avenue of the Americas New York, NY 10020

[27] McCullough, John Adams, pg. 406

[28] *John Adams* Episode 4 "Reunion" HBO Films, High Noon Productions, Playtone, Mid Atlantic Films 2008

[29] Jefferson, Thomas Letter to Francis Walker Gilmer June 7, 1816 from *The Works of Thomas Jefferson* edited by Paul Leicester Ford G.P. Putnam's Sons New York and London The Knickerbocker Press 1905 pg. 533-34

[30] Jefferson, Notes on Virginia Query XVII from *Jefferson Writings* pg. 285.

[31] Ibid.

[32] Dilorenzo, Thomas Hamilton's Curse: How Jefferson's Archenemy Betrayed the American Revolution – and What It means for Americans Today Crown Forum New York, NY 2008 pg. 4

[33] Jefferson, Thomas Letter to Judge Spencer Roane September 6, 1819 from *Jefferson Writings* pg. 1425

[34] Jefferson, Thomas First Inaugural Address from *Jefferson Writings* pgs. 522

[35] Jefferson, Thomas Second Inaugural Address from *Jefferson Writings* pgs. 493-494

[36] Jefferson, Thomas Letter to Thomas Cooper November 29, 1802 from *Jefferson Writings* 1108

[37] Jefferson, Thomas Special Message on Gun Boats February 10, 1807 from *Jefferson Writings* pg. 539

[38] Jefferson, Thomas Special Message on Gun Boats February 10, 1807 from *Jefferson Writings* pgs. 541-42

[39] Bernstein, R.B.

[40] Jefferson, Thomas Report on the Commissioners for the University of Virginia August 4, 1818 from Jefferson Writings pgs. 459-460

[41] Confederate States of America – Georgia Secession Avalon Project Yale Law School http://avalon.law.yale.edu/19th_century/csa_geosec.asp

[42] Lincoln, Abraham Conclusion of Lincoln's Last Speech in the Campaign of 1858 from *The Emergence of Lincoln: Prologue to Civil War 1859-1861* by Allan Nevins Charles Scribner's Sons New York, NY 1950 pg. 185.

[43] Lincoln, Abraham Letter to Horace Greeley August 22, 1862 from *Complete Works of Abraham Lincoln Volume XI* edited by John G. Nicolay and John Hay Francis D. Tandy Company New York 1905 pg. XIII

[44] *Two Treatises* pg. 79

[45] Lincoln, Abraham, Debate with Stephen Douglas, Sept. 18, 1858 from the National Park Service (U.S. Government) website http://www.nps.gov/liho/historyculture/debate4.htm

[46] A Declaration of the Immediate Causes which Induce and Justify the Secession of the State of Mississippi from the Federal Union The Avalon Project Yale Law School http://avalon.law.yale.edu/19th_century/csa_missec.asp

[47] Dilorenzo, Thomas *The Real Lincoln: A New Look at Abraham Lincoln, His Agenda, and an Unnecessary War* Three Rivers Press New York 2002 pg. 54

[48] Lincoln, Abraham First Political Speech at Pappsville, IL. – March 1832 from *Wit and Wisdom of Abraham Lincoln As Reflected in His Letters and Speeches* edited by H. Jack Lang Stackpole Books Mechanicsburg, PA 2006 (originally published by Greenberg Publishers New York 1941) pg. 1

[49] Lincoln, Abraham First Inaugural Address from The Avalon Project Yale Lillian Goldman Law Library http://avalon.law.yale.edu/19th_century/lincoln1.asp.

[50] Ibid

[51] McPherson, James M. *For Cause and Comrades: Why Men Fought in the Civil War* Oxford University Press 1997 pg. 18

[52] Bellows, Henry W. *Unconditional Loyalty* A.D.F. Randolph New York 1863 pg. 2 https://archive.org/stream/unconditionalloy00bell#page/2/mode/2up/search/sacred+person.

[53] Frederickson, George M. The Inner Civil War First Harper Torchbook edition published 1968 by Harper & Row, Publishers, Incorporated, New York, N.Y. 10016 pgs. 135-6.

[54] Genovese, Eugene "Religion in the Collapse of the American Union" from *Religion and the American Civil War* Oxford University Press 1998 Pg. 84

[55] Aristotle from The Politics and The Constitution of Athens edited by Stephen Everson Cambridge University Press New York, N.Y. 1996 pg. 17

[56] Dunbar, Seymour *A History of Travel in America* The Bobbs-Merrill Company Indianapolis, IN 1915 Volume I pg. 322

[57] Dilorenzo *How Capitalism Saved America* pg. 142